Language of the Stars in the City of Light

Anick Bourbonnière

Copyright (C) 2024 by Anick Bourbonnière

Book illustrated by the author

Original drawings starting at the age of six

ISBN: 9798218662905

The author's website: www.lightlanguage.co

Language of the Stars in the City of Light

In memory of my grandparents and all my ancestors,

Thank you!

Table of Contents

Thanks

I am immensely grateful to my wonderful children for their presence in my life. Their enriching experiences not only broadened my horizons, but also rekindled my childhood memories. An endless thank you to my husband for his support along the way. Your love, support and trust mean more than anything to me.

I am deeply grateful to Jean Casault for encouraging me to publish my story and for his constant support since my first public steps.

Thank you to my friend Evelyne Delude, editor and proof-reader, for her precious help in the development of my book. Her quest for understanding and her questions led me to further reflections and observations. She was able to capture the intangible and find the words when I lacked them.

Thank you to Cindy Thibault for laying the foundation of the book thanks to her expertise and dedication.

I would also like to thank Mary Rodwell, of Australia, for believing in me and giving me the confidence this past decade to continue to pursue the journey into the unknown.

In closing, I would like to thank the reading team: Isabelle Laflamme, Audrey Ducharme and David Boisvert.

Thank you all for being an integral part of this great journey.

Anick

Preface by Jean Casault

Anick Bourbonnière came into my life as the keynote of a symphony in the making. In 2016, I just started a series of radio shows at CJMD 96.9 FM in Lévis called Les Faits Maudits. To host a two-hour show on topics related to ufology and the paranormal (or deep ufology), you still have to deal with subjects that will capture attention. Doing it with a guest is almost a must.

And I made it a point not to have any guests on the phone unless it was really very far away.

Then suddenly I received an email that also captures more than my attention, it makes me shiver. You have to get up early to have that effect on me. Who is this great lady from elsewhere that I have here? Then, disappointed, I see that she lives in Calgary and this city is rather remote for me. But fate had it that Anick planned a trip to see her family in Quebec, exactly where I live, in St-Augustin-de-Desmaures. So, she accepts my invitation, and these will be moments that will be hard to forget.

In metaphysics, we call the energy released by a person or objects or places, the vibe, an English word derived from vibration. She was just that. Yes, there were her beautiful blue eyes surrounded by a growing wheat field, but I only had eyes on her pulsating sphere of energy and in my headphones, I had a song more than a voice. I let myself be lulled.

When she had finished the program with me on the theme of Blue Beings, I told her:

— "You, the Blue Being that you are."

I wasn't the first to tell her that. During an encounter with three Blue Beings, they will tell her:

— "Yes, Anick, you are part of us. You have always been a part of us. You can come back here with us at any time. This is your home here!"

I am not going to bore you with a long preface. The story of her life will be more than enough, so let's go with the best of the impossible, the deep ufology at its best, the incredible life of Anick Bourbonnière.

Introduction

The time has come to share with you the extraordinary journey I have experienced since I was a child. Unlike the heartbreaking adventures of many people claiming to have been abducted by otherworldly Beings, my encounters were marked by a sense of love and an unbreakable connection. Since I was born, I have been living a story of energetic and unconditional love. I felt heartbreak every time I had to return to Earth. The reminder of my life here seemed unbearable to me compared to my experience with them. It was only thanks to my husband and children that my life was forever transformed. They allowed me to embrace my Self on Earth. These precious people who make up my family, I have known them for eons. They share the same celestial origins of the New Earth. Thanks to our union, my twin souls, my divine counterparts, I have finally reconnected with the hidden memory of the City of Light, the cherished place of my youth. It was at the age of fifteen that I rediscovered its existence. As a result, the sense of my reality has changed.

My life took an unusual turn at the age of five following an event that reshaped the course of my life. This crucial ordeal was intentionally erased, ensuring that my life was not compromised by its influence. Over the years, memories have resurfaced, more specifically those of the age of eight. I will discuss them later in this book.

Since 2014, I have been aware of being a channel for transmitting galactic codes from the stars. I provide individuals with a personal connection to their galactic families. I facilitate their connection with the Beings of the New Earth. I simply serve as a conductor to this cosmic energy. Since my early childhood, my role on Earth has been to bridge the gap between our earthly realm and the world of our ancestors by passing on messages. In their realm they see beyond our linear time and thus can share insights about the evolution of our beloved planet.

I am fully aware that every individual I have met has played a vital role in my life. This includes my parents, sisters, and friends. I am also aware of the significant effect I have on the lives of many people through the stimulating wisdom of the Language of the Stars that I transmit. I am forbidden to reveal certain aspects of my background at this time. I recognize that people with malicious intentions have crossed my path. I feel that they are part of my destiny towards growth and enlightenment. Many people are selected with an intention that remains hidden from our consciousness, but the time for unveiling has come.

As you explore through the pages of my book, I ask that you to approach it with an open mind. You may discover that a part of you vibrates in this story. A sense of connection will forge. Our common history has only just begun. I hope that you will allow yourself to immerse yourself in this reality, which can be as complex as it is enlightening. It is a privilege for me to share these stories with you.

Chapter 1

Who am I

By day, I am a human being born on planet Earth in 1971. I cherish my life here on Earth. For me, being part of the human experience is a gift that has been given to all of us. I want to tell you to make the most of your life! Live life full of passion! Finding contentment in the small moments of our earthly existence is key. It is a precious gift to know or find the meaning of our presence on Earth. We should share it to help energize the planet. It took me a while to figure out how to use my "precious gift." I want to share with you what is invisible to make your soul resonate and to activate the parts of your being. I wish to allow you to fully embrace who you are through your adventure here.

My mission at night

However, at night, a profound transformation takes place. Still with my current body, I become a woman who has been around for hundreds of years. I work with a team in the City of Light. This place is dedicated to helping children from all over the world. In this city, I have a position in the medical section where I spend most of my time. My task is to transmit healing energies to them. I infuse them with codes of light and provide them with the necessary life energy if they need it. The Earth has a number of key stations for these children. One of them is in Ecuador. I get telepathic messages before they arrive. It's a privilege to be part of this incredible team. It's a timeless journey that connects my life during the day and my life at night.

Finally, home

I spent most of my childhood and adolescence in Quebec, Canada. Then, at the age of eighteen, I started exploring other continents. After a few years of working abroad, I returned to Canada, moving west to Alberta. Since 2021, I have been living in Ecuador with my husband and our two lovely children. My husband is Ecuadorian, but our love story began in 2004 in the Rocky Mountains of Western Canada. It was during our very first visit to his native country that something clicked in me. I feel a very strong connection with the Andes. This land calls out to me and creates a vibrant sensation to the depths of my being. These ancient mountains and mystical landscapes look like a piece of a puzzle that is missing from my life. I feel my soul awakening: a missing part of me has been found. I feel complete for the first time.

In 2014, my husband took us to the Chimborazo volcano. The closest thing on Earth to space. Everything is simply magical. An air of déjà vu envelops us: it's as if we've been there before. The energy of the volcano, with the large clouds and vast fields, surrounds us with infinite love. As in a dream, in an instant, we are drawn into a vortex of light. As we contemplate this splendid panorama, the City of Light comes to the fore. It's right there, in front of my children and me. My husband wonders what is going on with the children who have started to play. He does not discern what we see. This city has revealed itself in specific places throughout my life. It is a constant presence that guides my actions and decisions. It is also the heart of the book that you hold in your hands. From that moment on, I was certain that Ecuador was the place I needed to be from now on. This unique place was waiting for me.

In preparation mode

Before you start reading this book and dive into my story, I would suggest not to have any pre-established expectations. Certain things came to me in later years because my consciousness wasn't ready to accept or understand hidden information. Just like someone who goes through something traumatic doesn't fully remember the event. It will be blocked. But when your subconscious finally reveals itself and thinks it's time for you to understand it will communicate to your conscious self therefore revealing things you weren't consciously aware of previously.

Be sure to listen to the audio recordings through the QR codes provided. A QR code is a matrix symbol that leads to a Star Language recording designed especially for you. It prepares your consciousness to access the information transmitted to the soul throughout the book. Respect your feelings throughout reading these chapters. If necessary, take a break or reread some passages to integrate. Subtle changes may unfold in your life one by one afterwards. Just as it is possible that changes manifest themselves in an obvious way, or that emotional reactions rise out of nowhere (for our brain, but not for our being!). You just have to welcome and remain open towards yourself. And it is not because you do not feel anything at the time that nothing happens...

When you hold this book, it comes to life. Every page, sentence, and word is endowed with a shimmering energy that will enlighten your soul.

May the best be!

Discover your infinity!

YouTube: Light Language Ancestry

Chapter 2

My school beyond the sky

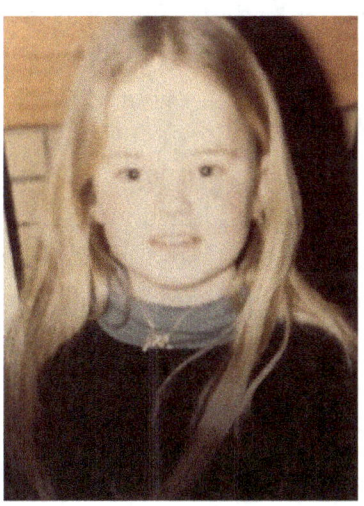

A new school year

I am only six years old and the memory remains vivid, as if it were yesterday. I am sitting on the carpet with my classmates. We are all gathered to listen to our teacher tell a magical story, carefully chosen to present our weekly lesson. Her stories are my favorite. In enchanting stories, I let myself get carried away with these adventures. I let my imagination and dreams run wild. On that day, something special happens. As our teacher's words fill the room, my body straightens up and I feel a part of my soul leaving. However, my physical form remains sitting on the mat. This new feeling is funny but very pleasant! I literally float on the ceiling. From this point of view, I see the students gathered around our teacher, absorbed in the story she is telling. No one sees me above their heads, no one notices that I am both sitting and outside my body... My thoughts are filled with panic yet settled. If no one sees me floating, what will happen? What if I don't come back into my body? And if I did not come back, my family would be worried. They are going to think I have left them. Will they forget about me? Maybe I'm getting kidnapped? Or maybe I am dying? I feel surrounded as if I were placed in a narrow and empty tube. In a burst of desperation, I muster up the courage to get their attention. The moment I want to scream, a soft and caressing energy of eternal and unconditional love runs through me and lulls me. The effect is so intense that I feel like I am falling asleep, but in truth, it's my consciousness that is flying to another world.

When I come back to awareness, I am in an unknown room, of immaculate white. There are children around me, but nothing here is like my school. There is no desk, and the students are replaced by new faces. Both in appearance and energy, these comrades are different. Fear grips me again. Immediately, the energy of pure love soothes me. Once calm and reassured, I can scan the surroundings again. Among the Beings of this multicolored group, only three of us come from Earth. How do I know? We have a striking resemblance. We have the same shapes of eyes, nose, mouth, arms, legs, feet, and hands. The other children have appearances that are far removed from earthly norms: blue, green, or even orange skin colors. Some have no mouth, have only one eye, or have a head that is oddly shaped to a human gaze. As I look at my new classmates, I realize that the other children come from a distant planet or star. Collectively, they form a mosaic of Beings from all over the universe. They all seem to share familiarities with each other. I feel like a complete stranger in their midst. I can't understand where I am, or what's going on. I can't help but feel different. My apprehensions resurface at high speed. Once again, a wave of appeasement filled with love and sweetness reduces my anxieties to pieces in the blink of an eye. This security allows me to connect to what is emerging in the room. Observing the other children, I notice that there is no need to be afraid.

In this particular place, there is a curious way of corresponding. We don't speak with words. Instead, we use what resonates in our energy as our common language: telepathy. This form of exchange is innate to our higher self, and young children like us use it to transmit all information. All codes of sounds, frequencies, and energy flow effortlessly between us. For my part, I naturally and effortlessly capture the words that are exchanged as if I had always been among them. Quite the opposite of the moment before, I feel an inexplicable well-being and belonging within this unusual class. At the same time, the light of my essence, of my soul, takes up all the space. I'm not six years old anymore, I don't have the awareness that I'm an Earthling who has a family and goes to school. These identifications no longer exist in my reality. My light, my unique essence, my soul, in short, who I Am takes all the space.

Then quickly, I find myself in my body, sitting in my seat in the classroom on Earth. I feel disoriented and lost in this rushed return in the middle of the routine at the end of the school day. I have to look at what others around me are doing to get my bearings. Since it takes me a long time to follow the instructions, my teacher comes to see me to make sure I'm okay. This is how a series of comments begin that will extend throughout my schooling:

— "Anick is often in the moon."

— "Anick has trouble staying focused."

— "Anick is often lost and constantly needs reminders for these tasks."

As I go on the spaceship almost every day, I miss a lot of academic learning on Earth. When my mother asks me what I learned during the day, I tell her that I don't remember. However, beautiful stories are happening beyond my awareness in my head. They are much more interesting than what happens with my teacher. My mother keeps telling me to make an effort and to listen when the teachers speak. I explain to her repeatedly that I don't mean to be in the moon. I get tired and that's when the knowledge unfolds in my head like dreams. Despite my efforts to try to stay attentive and do what the adults ask of me, I go back to "my dreams". I don't know why I'm different. I can't concentrate or follow the teachings. Since adults are not able to understand, they use the tools that they are familiar with. Nothing works. Crying in my bed, night after night, I beg the Moon very loudly. Since everyone says I'm in the moon, my perception was that it was me and the Moon's fault. But in reality they were talking about the concept of being "in the moon." Looking at it, I see a face. I ask it to make sure to allow me to stay attentive the next day at school, so I don't get grounded. I want to learn! I would like adults to stop being angry with me. I am sad to leave the spaceship. I'm sad to fail the Earth school subjects. It's complicated for me to follow the learning path. I'm so angry at the Moon for not accepting or even responding to my requests. It's hard for me to adapt.

My first discoveries

In the spaceship, I receive many teachings. These are moments of great discovery that are stored somewhere in my brain. They will be revealed a little later.

In the midst of this diverse assembly, the two teachers stand out from the group. One has an imposing figure with its slender blue shape with large black eyes. The other looks like an oversized green grasshopper, its build being incredibly delicate. Their looks have an air of admiration, further reinforcing the sense of unity that reigns in our circle. We all sit in a perfect circle. Around us, these two Beings walk gracefully and harmoniously clockwise. At the center is a mesmerizing source of energy: a radiant crystal ball that shines with the sparkle of a flaming diamond. It emits an energy of boundless love, abundance, and serene unity. This is unlike anything I have encountered on Earth. Through contact with this new energy, I can literally look and analyze the bodies of humans and animals. From then on, I can see through their physical forms to discern precisely what is going on in them. I dig beyond the surface, tracing what belongs to ancestral lineages back to about seven generations. In doing so, I absorb their energies and gain the ability to heal their pain and suffering.

I discover that each person I meet carries an invisible attachment that represents the interconnection between their past and parallel lives with their ancestors. This energetic cord is only broken when the individual successfully completes the learning that has remained unresolved. Imagine managing people's energy baggage at such a young age! I can predict the potential future of those I meet and know the likely consequences that await each individual. I also notice that each person gives off an energy of their own when a vibration passes through them. Simultaneously, a distinct color emerges. Each shade serves as a signature. It comes from the inner essence of the individual. It bears witness to the journey through the tapestry of existence. Reading emotions and their impacts in the body is part of my mission on the spaceship. The method of sharing information is quick and straightforward. I transmit what I have collected on Earth using a hologram projected by my third eye. The content of the scenes is "live", as if the students had been on Earth themselves. It is in this form that learning between classmates comes from.

In the spaceship, I notice that each of the students has a different mandate. In addition to the two Earthlings among us, there is a young girl my age. She has a well-defined responsibility: to ensure the well-being of all animals on the planet. She mentions that some of these are from different parts of the galaxy and that she is there to welcome them. The girl kindly reminds us that absolutely all creatures on Earth play an essential role in the balance of human energies. Without animals, human life on Earth would be unsustainable. This young girl's captivating ideas go even further. It does not support the popular belief that it is the evolution of animals that has implanted our world. She states that it is a deception perpetuated by science over the centuries. This young girl's mission is to travel to other planets in search of various animal species to advance Earthlings. Her knowledge and dedication are impressive.

The boy, a few years older than me, plays a major role in our group. He was given the task of managing the energy transfer of the complex technology of the various worlds used to speak with the other galaxies. Under his guidance, I began to understand how groups of stars merge to form galaxies across the vast expanse of the universe. He has the special ability to communicate with certain stars.

Although I cannot yet discern all the mandates of the other children, I perceive the bond that exists between the girl and the boy. Their energies resonate with mine. This makes it easier for me to feel the sophisticated interplay of their energies. Two years later, I meet a young girl from my school who bears a striking resemblance to the one in the spaceship. She's the same age as me. Intrigued, I approach her and ask her if she remembers our shared teachings. Her answer filled with surprise and confusion makes me realize that our memories about the spaceship are shrouded in a delicate veil when we return to Earth. I feel unique yet somewhat left out. The universe protects our fragile human minds from memories of our cosmic encounters that can prove confusing. This episode led me to realize that she might not have been the same girl.

Even though I am delighted by all these wonderful discoveries, my feelings are mixed. I am privileged to experience such things, but I am falling behind in the teachings of my earthly life, and it is causing me serious trouble. Thanks to the help of cosmic energies, I now excel in many subjects. With the exception of my first book in French (this Book), the language remains an eternal struggle for me. The cosmic and telepathic languages that reside in my mind seem to overshadow my ability to grasp this human language. In their support, my parents strongly disagree with the use of medication to improve concentration. Thanks to their unwavering support, I continue to fully explore the various spheres of my life as a child.

My training continues

Every day, I go back to that amazing classroom aboard the spaceship. It's a fantastic place to learn. I can educate myself and help others gain a deeper understanding of humanity. These lessons are conducted with discretion and are aimed at the evolution of planet Earth in the future. I cherish the time I spend on the ship. I am nostalgic every time I have to return to my earthly classroom. The time constraints of the physical world weigh heavily on me.

On the spaceship, I get to know the other children better. We are grouped by age categories: two to six years old, six to twelve years old and twelve to eighteen years old. Although I recognize myself as one of the youngest, I am curious to know what the older group is learning. What fascinates me is that each of us is accompanied by a Being who comes from a different galaxy. The Being plays a guardian role. Our supervisors are part of the older group. It is part of their task to take care of the youngest in the spaceship. Our protectors are appointed to us as soon as we arrive. I don't have the ability to clearly perceive the guides of others around me. However, a close link is woven between my Being and me. Its silhouette is an illuminated sky blue. He is about my height. He has a thin mouth; his intriguing look is blue, and his eyes are black. The more I observe, the more I notice a blueish green globe piercing out. My guide exudes incredible charisma. We share our thoughts, feelings, and ideas telepathically. As I navigate this fabulous journey of knowledge and transformation, he ensures my well-being by following me everywhere.

A disconcerting discovery

One day, I am walking near a long corridor in the spaceship. I notice that my Blue Being is no longer by my side. With my mischievous and adventurous spirit, I seize the opportunity and silently enter this unknown white passage. I stop at a door leading to a room covered in, once again, in immaculate white. The view that is offered to me is most intriguing. I feel like I'm in Santa's workshop! The room is filled with what at first appears to be dolls. The scene leaves me speechless. I wonder why all the figurines are the same and encased in these transparent tubes filled with a liquid that looks like water... Each tube is connected by a transparent, glittering cord. It carries energy, sound, vibrations, codes, and symbols. It's a similar form of communication to what I learn on the spaceship. This energy also enters through the top of my head and spreads through my body like a waterfall. The Language of the Stars is triggered inside me (at this moment, I don't know what it is, but I am aware of it) and suddenly I felt a merging sensation with the All and the infinite.

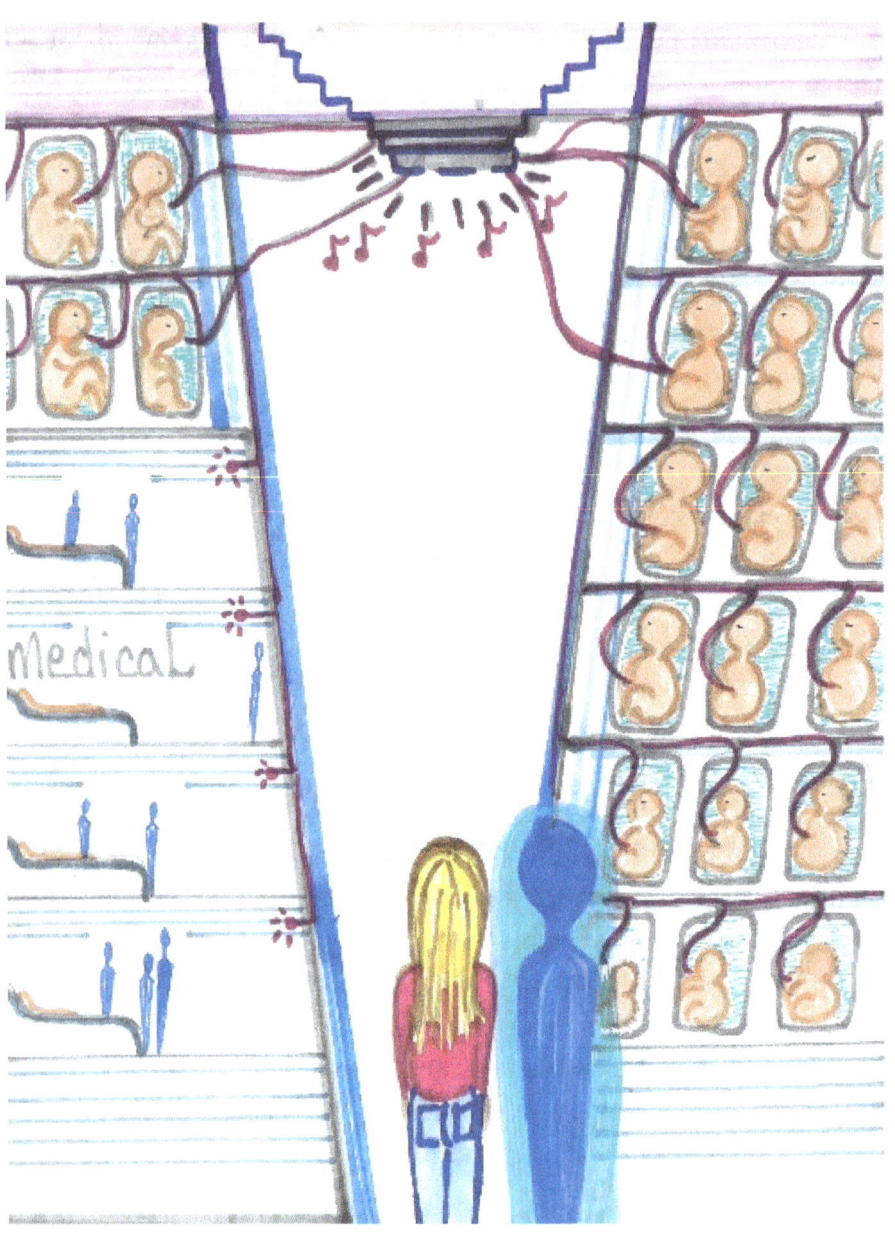

The magical energy and beauty that envelops these "baby dolls" charms me. In the distance, I observe two humans gently cradling two of them. I don't understand the meaning or purpose of what I see. Suddenly, my Blue Being appears and interrupts my exploration:

— "Where have you been? You don't have the right to venture alone, Anick," he warns me.

We leave the forbidden zone. My face flashes a euphoric smile from having explored mysteries. I can't wait to see what other no-go zones have in store for me. The lights flicker as we walk forward into the spaceship. There are countless doors. Every time we approach an opening, I am shrouded with excitement. One of the doors opens as we pass.

In response to my curiosity, a sudden unknown energy pushes me inwards. My entrance into the room is fast. My Being tried to hold me back without success. Surprised by the presence of my energy, four dazzling Blue Beings raise their heads in my direction. I can see that they are surrounding a person. My heart is pounding as I approach to see what is going on. As it was too late to try to hide the scene, hesitating, they let me approach. I recognize the silhouette of a woman lying on a bed. A sheet covers her prominent belly. Strangely, I feel a very familiar energy. Here I am very close to the bed. Looking at the face, I recognize my mother! The shock of this realization makes me tremble. In an instant, I find myself at my desk in my earthly classroom. When I came back this time I was disoriented.

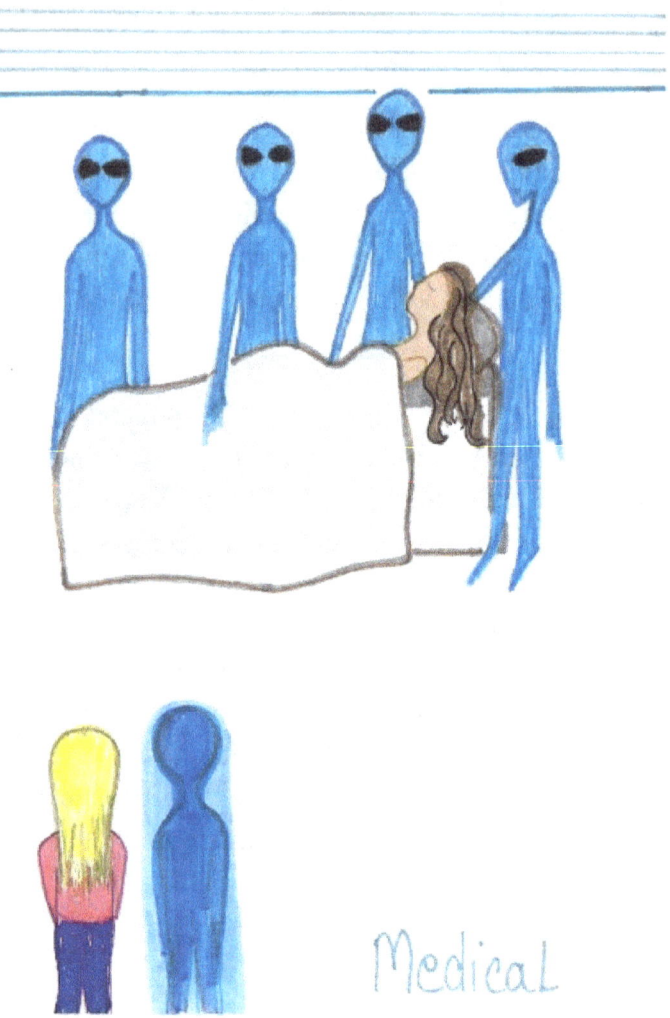

Medical

Once I got home, I looked at my mother in a different light...

The next day, when I returned to the spaceship, I felt a little anxious. I notice that the Blue Being and the Green Mantis pay special attention to me. They send me information about my mom's experience in the forbidden section. A warm energy circulates in my body, between my eyes, in my solar plexus and especially in my heart. They give me a holographic message that only I can perceive. Now I understand. My mother and other ancestors from various generations voluntarily committed themselves to this mission before their incarnation. They are usually no longer aware of these agreements, nor of the moments of absence or time spent in the vessels. They carry hybrid babies until they are perfectly formed. Then, they are removed from them and placed in see-through containers filled with a certain liquid. (So, the dolls are in fact babies, hybrid babies) I'm only six years old, so this process seems normal to me. I don't ask too many questions, because I don't understand the full extent of what is happening.

Year after year, my thinking about this view will mature and the information that comes to me will fit together like pieces of a puzzle. I will come to the conclusion that the Beings of the spaceship orchestrated the scene with my mother in the medical section so that I could witness it. Why? I would not discover it until many years later.

My advanced training: Energy and its use

In my perception of the world, the human body reflects the entire universe. The nervous system serves as a channel for me to connect to the multiple networks of oxygen, blood, cells, and organs that make up this living space. Every emotion I encounter represents a definite link with the past and parallel lives of individuals. Very often, it is directly linked to their ancestral lineages. For example, when a person feels anger, a navy-blue hue surrounds their figure and a specific region of their body is affected. I can discern everything with remarkable precision, down to the most affected organ, like the liver in this case. It is through the vibrational reaction of emotions that I understand how they affect a person's health in a negative way. Thanks to these observations, I understand why some children and adolescents suffer from illnesses or episodes of depression throughout their lives. These energetic dynamics are subtle. I have noticed that children and adolescents who protect themselves from their parents' arguments can develop ear infections.

Similarly, those who choose to close their eyes to the unseen, avoid the unknown, or resist what comes their way may develop a decrease in their eyesight until they need glasses. Emotions are inscribed in the body, modifying their life and well-being more or less consciously. Sometimes, it is the vibrations from the character traits inherited from the family clan that are activated during stress or anger.

When I try to share this knowledge with those around me, I am not heard. No one pays attention to a child who brings up topics that we think are out of her reach and that adults are not able to perceive.

In addition, the transfer of energy can be done from parents to children or between siblings. The colors around individuals can change in response to their emotions, reflecting the flow of their states of mind. Vibrant hues reflect happiness and softness. However, I focus on the relationships of children and adolescents with their parents or the adults in their lives. It is in this specific area that I devote my abilities.

I learn why children and teenagers have an innate ability to absorb negative energies. It's a mechanism that looks a lot like an intuitive sponge. The purpose of this process is to protect their parents from unhappiness, sadness, or illness. In fact, this is the unspoken mission of children on Earth. Subsequently, the young transmute into nature what they have absorbed and learned. If they do not have the opportunity to effectively discharge these energies with the help of nature, they are at risk of developing anxiety, depression, behavioral disorders, or hyperactivity. Children are therefore intrinsically linked to the Earth. The balance is maintained through their interactions with rocks, insects, water, trees, and wind. These natural elements allow them to free themselves from the burdens they carry and recharge their batteries with the powerful energy of the Earth. Over the years, for many children, the connection with nature has weakened, and practically broken. The main reasons are changes in lifestyle habits as well as the fear of being teased by peers if they let themselves go freely.

Chapter 3

Here on Earth

Meeting my grandfather

My youth was spent in the French-speaking province of Quebec, located in Eastern Canada. My childhood was rooted in a small village called St-Augustin-de-Desmaures. It is in a humble two-storey house on the banks of the St. Lawrence River that I meet the paranormal world. The house itself is home to spirits who also make it their home.

At the age of eight, the death of my maternal grandfather was a turning point in my life. This moment is an important aspect that has repercussions on my destiny. This death allows me to reconnect with the spirits of my ancestors and to glimpse the mysteries of the afterlife. My grandfather comes from an Indigenous heritage, more specifically the Mig'mawag, or Mi'kmaq; a lineage that has been going on for many generations. My dearest grandfather has distinctive physical traits. He has a slender figure, slightly reddish skin, dark brown slanted eyes and black, straight hair combed back. I have a great affinity with him. It's like I've known him for ages. This grounded connection leads us to believe in the possibility of karmic connections. I know for what purpose we choose our parents before we incarnate. It is through these connections that we attract people who are instrumental in addressing the karma of other lifetimes. This connection, rekindled with my ancestral roots, making me explore the richness of my heritage from the Mig'mawag people.

In Saint-Augustin, as in the vast majority of villages in Quebec, the school, the church and the cemetery are neighbors. My daily commute to school takes me right across the street from the cemetery. It was during one of these walks that an unimaginable encounter occurred: there, in front of me, stood my grandfather. That same grandfather that everyone says is dead. His presence surprised me and filled me with joy. In a tender voice, he confides in me that he is with me from now on. At eight years old, I don't fully understand this exceptional encounter, but I trust my intuition. I don't understand him being dead. I guess he's like the spirits in my house and just comes to visit me for a short while because he's feeling lonely. However, it soon became clear that he is not just visiting me for a brief moment. He is constantly there to guide me. He always stands in the same place every morning when I go to school. The bus stop is not located on the school grounds: it is located in the church parking lot next to the cemetery. My grandfather accompanies me from the bus to the entrance of my classroom safely. He becomes the wise guide of my life and offers me clarification on the unusual path I have traveled and that I will travel in the coming years. His teachings are transformative. They reshape my perspective on the present, the past, and the future.

There are days when I wish I could chat with my friends without his watchful presence. Respectful and understanding, he remains discreet. One day, as I was getting ready to leave, I asked him to accompany me to see my mother. He refuses, simply stating that it is not the right time, because my mother would not be ready to understand the meaning and purpose of our exchanges. My grandfather also plays the role of tutor. He carefully teaches and guides me through the rules and steps necessary to cross the veil that separates the visible and invisible worlds. Thanks to him, I became more comfortable with realms beyond our physical reality. At his side, I benefit from a comforting entry into this parallel dimension. Every day, my grandfather tests and advises me, preparing me for the subtleties of the invisible dimensions. My mind is not often present in class. When I'm not in my other school in the spaceship, I'm here on an "internship". I solve the problems of my classmates' ancestors that their parents didn't solve. Or I am busy traveling and receiving my grandfather's teachings in the intersection of the timelines of the past and the future. I am aware of the importance of these lessons. I constantly have to catch up on what I missed in the evening before bedtime. To support me in my school here on Earth, he gives me dictations and texts to compose in order to practice and improve my grades. This episode in my life, based on the unbreakable bond between my grandfather and me, contains an array of emotions and wonder.

What I'm going through is something that no one else can really understand. Over time, through these experiences, my connection with the spiritual and ancestral worlds deepens and transforms my life in a permanent way. I am increasingly able to transcend the boundaries of life and death. The ability to bridge the gap between the world of the living and the world of spirits, has been a secret that has been hidden for a very long time. It is shared only with certain descendants of my grandfather who also have this ability. I have the privilege of knowing the Indigenous ancestors of our land. I even meet my grandfather's great-grandfather. He is a man with a remarkable figure who lived near the hill overlooking the St. Lawrence River. I recognize his impressive presence by the lingering smell of the tobacco he smokes. Also, the resemblance to my grandfather's younger portrait is striking. This third great-grandfather describes the St. Lawrence River as the "Great River of Waters" and says that he shares an intimate connection with nature and water. He later reveals to me that the indigenous people call it the Magtogoek River which translates to "the river of great waters". He speaks to the river as if water and nature were gods. This revelation impresses me.

I spend a lot of time outdoors, absorbing the teachings of my Indigenous ancestors by witnessing their sacred dances and songs that have the power to mesmerize the entire village. And the only living earthling who notices them is me. My grandfather explains to me that the Iroquoians also made this hill their home. He tells me that his great-grandfather had been in love with an Iroquoian woman. Unfortunately, this was forbidden by tradition. The details have not been revealed to me yet, which makes this part of the story that surrounds me even more touching. Back on the property where I grew up, I often hear melodies carried by the water and the wind. When I think about them, they fill me with warmth and nostalgia. By breathing deeply, I can relive my precious childhood memories at this age.

On the way to school

One school day, as I walk past the cemetery, something entirely new and startling happens:

— "Anick! Anick!" shouts a voice.

I try to locate the source of this call, but I don't see anyone. In the distance, my grandfather appears. He moves calmly towards me. I thought it must be his voice, so I keep walking. The voice persists, calling me again and again. As I approach the cemetery, I begin to discern transparent silhouettes, a bit like the first time I saw my grandfather. The closer I get, the clearer they become, even if they remain somewhat translucent. These shapes are intriguing because their faces and feet are hidden. It seems that they are concealing something, they are embarrassed or ashamed. The specters behave as if they are showing themselves for the first time in decades, if not centuries. I feel like I'm turning heads in my path. Maybe I'm getting too much attention! It was then that my grandfather quickly approached to reassure me.

⸺ "She's not ready yet! She is much too young! We have to wait to contact her, he exclaims to the spirits of the cemetery."

They have long since passed into the realm of the dead, and their presence weighs heavily upon my young heart. Despite the unsettling nature of their appearances, I feel a rather inexplicable affinity with them. We seem to share a bond through my ability to straddle the energetic boundaries of life and death. The meeting with the inhabitants of the cemetery left me both curious and a little frightened. I don't understand everything that's going on. As the day continues, I am playing in the playground with my friends. Suddenly, my mind is racing again: I hear the call of my name in the distance. I'm reluctant to draw attention to myself in the playground... I'm hesitant to take a look at the cemetery, but I can't help but do so. It is at this moment that I have a strange encounter. To my surprise, a small figure appeared next to me. It's a young boy of about five or six years old looking at me.

⸺ "So, you can see me! The others there have been watching you for a month" he tells me.

I was surprised, and I didn't answer right away. I fear the reactions of the children around me which may think that I am talking to myself. I am also worried about the hundreds of deceased who lie further away there and who have been asked to wait to contact me. The young boy introduces himself as Hugo. I avoid giving him attention as much as possible. I don't have permission to come into contact with the deceased. He informs me that all the others are curious about the new girl in the village who can see and talk to them. He mentions that I have been awaited for a long time. I long for my grandfather's presence. I don't feel his energy around. It's rather reassuring to know that he's always close to me when I'm at school... But where are you grandpa?

The bell rings and pulls me out of my thoughts about Hugo and the cemetery. I look around, relieved that Hugo is no longer there. I sit down at my desk and think back to the curious encounter I had. Hugo, by the innocence of his young age, probably does not suspect that he is in the cemetery. My grandfather explains some of the rules of the spirit world to me. Some time ago, he mentioned that deceased people can appear differently. It is often because they have not yet understood that they are no longer in our earthly world. Wandering around us, a little lost, sad and confused, they want to inform us of their presence. They do not understand that a thick veil prevents us from seeing them. I have great empathy for these lost souls in their incomprehension when they try to get the attention of the living. It's heartbreaking to think that they keep asking themselves why they go unnoticed.

One thing is curios: for two days, I have not received any news from my grandfather or Hugo. I wonder where they are. Maybe they went on a trip or just decided to let me play alone with my friends. At school, I can see the ethereal company of my classmates and teacher. Some guides stand at a distance behind them, and others come and go providing silent support or valuable advice. Everyone has their own spiritual companions in the same way I have my grandfather. Nevertheless, it seems obvious to me that my friends are totally unaware of the presence of these benevolent guides in their lives.

A few days later, still on my way to school, Hugo joined me with the cemetery crowd. My grandfather was not present that day. I feel vulnerable and worried as they gather around me, studying me as if I was from another world. Hugo wants to comfort me by assuring me that they are friendly. They all have their own set of questions. Some of them ask me if I can pass on messages to their families. Suddenly, I see my grandfather approaching us. He addresses the group and politely asks them to respect the laws governing our interdimensional interaction. He reiterates the fact that I am not ready for such a demanding match. They all nod and disappear except for Hugo. I watch with fascination my grandfather chat with him warmly. My grandfather asks Hugo to leave. His grandparents are waiting for him at the cemetery gate. Then he leaves. My grandfather approaches me. I ask him why this boy lingered in this place. He tells me that Hugo's mother used to go there regularly to converse with her parents. He died at the age of five following an illness. It was the only place the young boy knew. It gave him a sense of security by being with his grandparents. Our conversation ends as we take the road back to school. Once again, my connection with the spiritual world is strengthened by this magnificent experience led with gentleness and firmness by my beloved grandfather.

Hugo and I have forged a special bond. Our conversations are filled with learning. My new friend shares his knowledge with me. He teaches me important lessons about life and existence. There was a moment when I felt overwhelmed. I was discouraged by the difficulties at school and the lack of understanding of the adults and teachers around me. Hugo, who knows that I attend the interstellar school on the spaceship, sympathizes with my difficulties. To help me, he whispers words to me in advance while I am reading in class. Even though he is younger than me, he reveals to me that in one of his lives, he had worked with books for a long time. He explains to me the eternal nature of life and the concept of reincarnation. Which leaves me curious as to why he hasn't reincarnated. Hugo also introduced me to the notion of manipulating energy in future lives, a concept that left me perplexed at the time. In our moments of escape, Hugo and I read books together and explore other dimensions. We spend hours looking at the pictures and stories in the Martine's books[1]. I was blessed by his presence in my life for two years. It was a real privilege. I am eternally grateful for all the knowledge and company he has given me. He came to say a final goodbye to me when I was ten years old. He was happy to share with me that he was embarking on a new mission. I have never seen him since. I often wonder if he was reincarnated or if he moved on to another mystical realm. I hope that one day, I will feel its comforting and enlightening energy surrounding me again.

Since those years, I have been conversing regularly with the spirits of the elderly in the cemetery. These encounters allowed me to travel into their world and hear stories from the good old days that they cherish. I can even perceive the invisible links that unite them to their ancestors.

Valuable advice

My grandfather has a keen sense of my surroundings and watches over me relentlessly. I constantly feel his energy close to me. He doesn't venture too far or for too long. He protects me in several areas. His advice takes the form of intuitive, whispered messages in the ear.

I remember very well the time when, at school, we were given little envelopes of fluoride in class. It was claimed that rinsing our mouth with this product was beneficial for the health our teeth. My grandfather warned me not to touch this liquid.

— "But why, grandpa?" I ask him. "I want to be like my friends."

---

[1] French Collection Books started in 1954 by Belgian authors Gilbert Delahaye and Marcel Marlier

⊢ "Sell them for 25 cents. Don't put them in your mouth. This is very bad, even dangerous." He responds detecting the energy of the harmful chemicals.

Here are some other examples: Once, he asked me to tell my mother not to drink tap water. He detected the presence of toxic substances. My mother followed the advice without questioning its source. A few months later, a tragic revelation struck our village when several young people were diagnosed with leukemia. It turned out that our water supply had been contaminated. The authorities have never exposed the whole truth about its toxicity.

On many occasions, he told me not to eat certain foods. They would have made me sick. He insisted on using a blanket between the grass and me instead of lying directly on the grass behind our house. The lawn contained pesticides.

At other times, his warnings have proven invaluable in ensuring the well-being of my entire family. For example, staying away from certain people my father met. I could name several occasions. Here are two situations that could have been particularly perilous. During a trip in our RV, my grandfather gives me an alternative route to pass on to my father. He knows something is not right. It was a safer choice than the initial route. My father is receptive to my instructions and follows the advice. I am grateful that my grandfather is there to protect us.

Finally, at the age of nine, we are on our way to Disney World in Florida. Our van broke down on the highway. I remember being disappointed because I didn't want to miss anything. What were the chances that the failure would occur at this exact location on this route? The orchestration of this scene by my grandfather was simply destined once again. About 20 minutes later, a plane crashed into the icy Potomac River after striking the 14th street bridge on the same highway a few miles in front of us. About a hundred people lost their lives. We later realized that if we had continued our journey, we could have been caught in this terrible accident. This story persists even today in our family conversations. A disappointing outcome at first glance that a breakdown prevents us from arriving at our destination as planned. What a relief and gratitude for this intervention that literally saved our lives that day.

Chapter 4

Our inhabited house

Our home is located on an expansive plot of land on top of a majestic hill. My room is on the upper floor, right next to my parents. This pleasant sanctuary is a little larger than those of my two younger sisters. I feel exceptionally lucky. From my window, I have the privilege of contemplating the expanse of the river and its meanders. The view is like a painted canvas. Every morning, the curtains filter the first rays of the sun and I wake up to the sound of the sweet melody of the birds. What a joy it is to wake up in this haven of serenity that is mine! I feel immense gratitude for this. It is in this sweet refuge that I can seek comfort at any time. Despite this tranquility, a special aura floats in my room. Like many rooms in old houses, a small trapdoor on the ceiling provides an entrance to the attic. Every time I pass in front of this door, I see a luminous tunnel that invites me to enter it. This portal doesn't scare me. Rather, it is an intriguing gateway to the unknown. During the day, I hesitate to enter it. Despite my great curiosity, I don't venture. However, as night falls, the attraction to this radiant opening increases. My resistance is diminishing. Finally, filled with apprehension and anticipation, I venture out to discover this energetic field.

My sister, who is seven years younger than me, regularly joins me in the evenings. She is reluctant to sleep in her room because she does not feel comfortable. We face the dimensional mysteries of the night together. The possibilities are endless. We share parallel universes and experience similar phenomena. I am acutely aware of what happens during our nightly travels, while my sister doesn't remember it. Our joint explorations into the invisible world, via this luminous path, strengthen the strong inexplicable bond between us since her first breath. I have a strong instinctive need to protect her. On every excursion, I find it comforting to know that she is with me or physically safe in my bed. When the luminous door opens to us, the depth of love beyond measure floods me completely. Love is a force that binds us to each other, no matter what world or dimension we find ourselves in. In this case, I feel like my sister's fate and mine are intimately linked. Since then, things have changed and the life course specific to each of us has distanced this once close relationship.

Moreover, one night, when the household is sinking into sleep, I energetically detect my mother going through the vortex of light. She travels alongside a huge Insect Being! This vision causes a shiver of terror in me, forcing me to return to the safety of my sheets. This experience is incomprehensible. As a form of protection, denial activates to calm the brain of the young human that I am.

In many corners

Truth be told, my family is not the only occupant of our residence. The attic is home to an entire family of spirits. They made me understand that this is indeed theirs. Surprisingly, I welcome their presence thinking that everyone sees what I see. It was a time when I still didn't realize that I was different from the other children in the village and from my family members. The presence of these ghostly people is a normal facet of my childhood. I find comfort in their company. The shimmering portal presents itself as a gateway between the two worlds. Sometimes I have the honour of having several generations of the same family visit. These ancestors gathered together and solemnly stand by my bed. Their faces reflect the wisdom of their age. Peaceful, they observe me intensely, sometimes exchanging words with each other in low voices. I don't feel threatened. There is an inexplicable serenity in their presence. This absence of malevolence relieves my mind.

The steps of the staircase that lead upstairs are also a place frequented by inhabitants of the supernatural domain. I was about twelve years old when I met ghostly soldiers. They appear for the first time sitting on the stairs. They all greet me. As we ascend the creaky staircase that leads to my room, the members of the army take up their positions as guards of honor: a salute of respect with their rifles pointed high on the left shoulder. Day after day, these solemn sentinels nod their heads in recognition as I pass them. This endearing routine brings an atmosphere of camaraderie to this unconventional environment. Their presence feeds my sense of comfort in this house full of mysteries. This episode coincides with the time when my father brought back an imposing photo of my grandfather's regiment. The people who appear in it have mostly died. But my mother doesn't want to display a memory that we hardly know anyone about. She asks my father to get rid of it. The latter, who did not want to part with it, hung the photo behind the piano inherited from his paternal grandmother. That's what caused these soldier spirits to remain in my house!

The characteristic atmosphere of our house comes from my father's antique collection. Each object contains a cumulative energy of its experience. It is not surprising that these apparitions take place here. The furniture itself contains ancient stories just waiting to be revealed. Unbeknownst to my father about this fact, a disturbing cold gradually permeates our family. An unpleasant climate gradually takes hold of the house, affecting our collective mental well-being. Year after year, I can feel the unfriendly energy growing in the rooms lined with old furniture carrying their past. This unfortunate transformation alters the essence of our once pleasant home. The attic, a sanctuary for my friends of the unknown, loses its shine and the luminous vortex fades away. With each passing day, my dreams become more and more disagreeable.

Chapter 5

The City of Light

YouTube: Light Language Ancestry

Extra-sensory information

I am fifteen years old. As a summer job, I work in Quebec City, not far from one of the most wonderful places: Le Petit Champlain. My uncle is the owner of the nautical clothing store. The customers are mainly tourists who arrive by boat to visit Old Quebec. My heart has long been captivated by the world of fashion. It's a job that fills my days with a mix of conscientious work and passion. This opportunity allows me to immerse myself in its vibrant matter, literally. Let me explain...

I have a curious innate sense that sets me apart from others in this field. I have the ability to feel the energy of the people and the human touch that has made every garment in the store. I connect as much with the material as with the energy of the designers, who sometimes take several turns to create a piece. The awareness of these elements runs through me and I can discern whether the employees have suffered injustices during manufacturing. The emotions that emanate from it are as varied as the stories woven on each thread. There is the pride of the craftsmen who make with love, but also the anguish of those who work in oppressive conditions. It's a reminder that the world of fashion is not just about beauty: the suffering related to the exploitation and poor conditions of workers, both children and adults, is very real. This sensitivity pushes me to better understand the impact of my choices as a consumer. This gift extends beyond the workplace. I am unable to put on clothes that have belonged to others, even after they have been thoroughly washed. The energy of emotions and handling present in the fabric remains tangible to me. I absorb all their vibrations, both the sweetness and the pain. This somewhat invasive ability regularly overwhelms me. As a child, I struggled with the same situation when it came to wearing second-hand clothes. It is impossible for me to ignore the resonance of past vibrational imprints. It's a difficult day-to-day management. Sometimes it feels like an ordeal. However, this ability to receive information in this way brings me back to what life on Earth is like, that is to say a multitude of experiences that follow one another.

The legacy of the family clothing business has long been in the family's veins. It is a tradition carefully cultivated over the generations: from my great-grandfather to my grandfather and then to my father. In the air, implicitly float around me, great expectations directly related to entrepreneurship: it is expected that I in turn take up the torch of the business and continue the already established notoriety.

Stand on my own two feet

As a teenager, I am no different from my peers. I long for the camaraderie of friends, to go out on weekends and revel in the thrill of youth! My grandfather, a figure of wisdom, still gives me advice. He urges me to be careful, but above all to rest and soak up the energy of the sun. Now, the exuberance and carelessness of youth make me ignore him. I am becoming more and more rebellious; I want to taste a "normal" life as my friends seem to enjoy it. One day, I found the courage to express my desire for independence to my grandfather:

— "Grandpa, I love you, but I need to start living my life the way I want to now. I don't want you to tell me what to do anymore."

My statement casts a heavy silence in the air. My unequivocal affirmation jumps in the echo of my voice being heard for the first time. I want to stand on my own two feet. I have to counter this benevolent but very supervised guidance in order to allow me to make my own itinerary. My grandfather, in his unconditional love and full of understanding, looks me in the eye:

— "I understand, Anick" he says, nodding.

From that moment on, he graciously withdraws, allowing me to chart my own path and make my own decisions without his directions. I still feel the presence of my invisible guardian, someone I can always count on in times of need. It's a comforting safety net that doesn't disappear entirely. I am thus exploring my freedom. It tastes exhilarating, but it comes with its share of challenges... I set out on my conquest by imitating my friends to discover the world in the same way as they are doing. I still feel like a foreigner. I remain unique in many ways. There are times when I wish for the comfort of my room, where I can find myself alone with my thoughts, far from the clamor of the world. Moreover, my courtyard with the view of the majestic river remains a sanctuary in which I lose myself in contemplation. I am looking for answers to the question of my reason for being.

A stunning appearance

My life takes place in the comforting cocoon of a relatively wealthy family. My mother plays the role of a housewife while my father works on the road as a representative in the clothing industry. His territory extends throughout the province of Quebec. He is therefore often absent for several consecutive days. Even at that time, I enjoyed the peacefulness of life on the banks of the St. Lawrence River. I have the chance to admire the lovely sunrises and sunsets. This rhythm of time that unfolds before my eyes is synonymous with pure magic. The cascade of energy that emanates from the elements of nature is a pure, tender, nourishing connection that reminds me that I belong in this universe. It encourages me to persevere and pursue the quest for who I am.

Yet, within the serene confines of our home, my life is punctuated by moments when the air becomes heavy and the tension certain. I still feel the emotional frequencies of absolutely everything around me: my parents and my two sisters, the house, and its contents. During these moments, I try to escape from them, to find comfort and to free myself from these overloads. Instinctively, it is in the arms of nature that I find the exquisite embrace I need. One morning in July, the calm of our house is disrupted by my father's return. His presence, a force of nature, does not go unnoticed:

— "The future belongs to those who get up early!" He excitedly declares as the sun begins to rise. It was the signal to start our day.

That morning, it is the aroma of the coffee he is preparing and spreading in the air that wakes me up. With his usual zeal, his voice resounds everywhere:

— "Come on, everyone up!"

Family members come alive in response to his call. A new day takes shape with its possibilities, its troubles and its shared moments of love and connection. I wake myself from sleep and reluctantly get up from my bed, the weariness etched on my face. With a heavy heart, seeking respite from the busy atmosphere of the morning, I head to the back of the house and walk through the patio door. The silent courtyard attracts me. That morning, the sky was grey and the nature around me gave off a sense of calm. The wind gently brushes against my hair. Despite the clouds that veil the sun, I can clearly feel its presence by the warmth on my skin. The humid air exerts a lot of pressure, making every breath an ordeal. I go down the steps that lead to the pool. The scent of the surrounding multicolored trees and flowers is sweet. It soothes and vitalizes my mind. Every step brings me closer to my favorite spot: a vast area of soft grass where I love to lie down. When I arrive at my destination, I sit down to gather my thoughts and let the fatigue dissipate. An intense melancholy brings me back to existential questions. Why am I here? What is the purpose of my life? Why am I so different compared to the others? How did I come to integrate into this life that is so complex for me? This whirlwind brings tears that slowly run down my cheeks. I close my eyes to try to chase away the cloud laden with uncertainties that hovers over me. A few moments later, a slight fizz under my eyelids, which are still closed, pushes me to open my eyes. Through a vision blurred by tears, a strange phenomenon appears. An unearthly mist forms in the distance in front of me. I blink to focus. I gradually catch a glimpse of a massive, circular, metallic shape suspended in the sky. At first, I mistake this oval platform for clouds. As my eyes squint against the bright light, I realize that these are not clouds at all. I can clearly see a gigantic structure floating above the river. It has a transparent dome. I stare in amazement at this surrealist object that goes beyond the laws of physics. My mind flickers in disbelief. My logic is repelled by the information that my senses send me. I wonder what this is all about.

In the space of a few seconds, it is as if I were reconnecting with a parallel existence in which there is a fusion of past and future. In the time it takes to breathe, what is in front of my eyes slowly fades away. Nothing in the air anymore: everything is gone! Shaken by the vision, I cannot begin to doubt the authenticity of what I have just witnessed. Was it real or was it a figment of my imagination? Immediately after, a distinct sensation unfolds in my body. Despite the extreme heat of the morning, a relentless cold runs down my spine. Suddenly, a headache grabs me and takes root in my temples. Weakness invades me, making my steps waver. I find the strength to go back to lie on my bed. A few days go by, and I continue to feel unwell. In fact, from time to time through my adolescence I feel inexplicable sadness. As my health slowly deteriorates the ghostly apparitions become unwelcomed companions. I am tired of their persistent presence. The ancestors who live in the house watch over me day and night. I'm trapped in a confusing world. I feel like I'm going through an endless parade of minds where the past intertwines with the present without a clear solution to address the future.

A second appearance

A few weeks passed. The general state of exhaustion is still there. This morning, I take advantage of a slight boost of energy to sit facing the St. Lawrence River. I am constantly drawn to the place where I saw the oval shape. With each deep breath, I try to soothe the discomfort of the uncertainty of what I had seen before. I hope to make sense of all this. Suddenly, just as miraculously as the first time, I see the oval shape appear. I squint my eyes to perceive better. To my great surprise, it is still there! This unforeseen spectacle once again leaves me with more questions than answers.

An intense vibration suddenly takes hold of me. A strange sensation runs through my body and my energy. Something is stirring inside. This strange vibration slowly rises in my interior, frees itself from my physical form and flies into the sky without limit. The emotion is so intense that it takes my breath away! I find myself freed from the constraints of space and time. In an instant, I am transported to the top of the gigantic sphere above the river. Between heaven and earth, I look with astonishment at a city from another world that materializes in front of me. Anxiously, I approach what looks like a transparent bubble. I am captivated to finally be able to discover by what I hoped so much to see again. It's unlike anything I've seen in my life! I feel like I'm in the "It's a Small World" ride at Disney World. The place is populated by young children. Some eyes have a youthful glow, while others where elderly containing the wisdom of the ages. Their frail frameworks symbolize a life well beyond a century. They are adorned with celestial, flowing, and silky garments that shimmer in the ambient light. Twirling serenely above this Secret City, I wonder if these little inhabitants are aware of my presence. Sometimes I get so close to them that I can hear them conversing in a language that is both foreign and familiar...

Suddenly, without understanding how or why, I lose all my senses, I effortlessly transform into a ball of radiant light that gracefully crosses the heavens. The feeling is exhilarating, and I want to linger for eternity! I am blown away by the incredible beauty. My unexpected experience ends as quickly as it began. The next moment, I rush back into my body in earthly matter. This return to reality leaves me in shock. The desire to regain the serenity and richness that I have just witnessed makes my heart sigh. This ephemeral adventure gives a boost of excitement in the midst of my dreary daily existence. The length of the stay in this other world is indeterminate. Who knows, a few seconds, minutes or more? In my consciousness, this episode opens up new perspectives on an alternative destiny.

The next morning, a fever takes hold of me. In this state, I don't know if my adventure in another world is real or not. Lying in bed, I oscillate between the boundaries of waking and dreaming. Is all this the product of my tiredness or am I really sick? The weakness of my body is intensifying day by day. As for my spirit, it seems to be rising, connecting to a higher power that transcends earthly limitations. I don't dare to resort to my grandfather. I fear that his presence will dissolve the chances of seeing this City of Light again that is beginning to change the course of my existence.

On the other side of the veil

The calendar is turning to September. Rather than going back to school, I am held captive in bed by my fatigue. My thoughts are consumed by the Luminous City that hypnotizes my heart and soul. It is a world of magic and fascination that has a magnetic appeal to me in my state of continual weakness.

During my loneliness, I find comfort in the company of the old souls who reside in my home. They entrust me with stories and memories that are dear to them. I quickly notice that when they look at my frail figure, my ethereal companions wonder where my grandfather is. In the days that follow, I get tired of being in my room. I head to the patio at the back of the house. I hope to be able to revisit the Enchanting City. The sun's rays pierce the clouds. Immediately, my mind frees itself from its earthly limitations. I gaze towards the horizon. I widen my eyes to see further in order to pierce the thin veil that separates me from the dimension of the floating city. Coming from everywhere at once, powerful undulations propel me immediately above the City!

As I examine the place, forms begin to be developed. Attentive, I scrutinize what is gradually revealed: children. They run happily through vast fields surrounded by lush trees, vibrant plants, and magnificent flowers. It is then that I too, at that moment, surprise myself by being able to smell the sweetness of each flowers' scent while I float in the air. The damp air and earth of the tropical gardens come to life before my eyes. Birds of all kinds fly all around and fill the atmosphere with vitality with their songs. A turquoise blue ocean shimmers further away. Its waves lap happily on the shores. Pink and blue-grey dolphins play in the water. All this grandiose landscape overwhelms my senses. A jungle teeming with animals is revealed. Multiple insects talk to each other telepathically. I see their conversations moving through the air. I capture their energies, their interactions, and the links between them.

It is difficult to find the words and to describe exactly how this incredible moment feels. I feel the transfer of energy between creatures, plants, and children as they wander around as they please. I am part of this exciting new world. I feel united with the energy of Life which is One. My own energy turns into light. I merge with, what I will discover later, another facet of my being. I no longer feel like a human being who travels to another dimension: I have an unlimited existence. I am an eternal woman, wonderful and intimately linked to what makes up existence.

To my great pleasure, my journey is prolonged. I fly peacefully to the edge of the noble forest. I see the children of the City holding stones and crystals as they connect with them. Thanks to these minerals, they absorb information in the form of frequencies. They then pass on this wisdom to the trees, the earth, and the planet itself. They are real transmitters of energy. Every word a child utters resonates in harmony absolutely everywhere and the trees turn to them. All knowledge can be stored in these crystals. I am fascinated by the communication between the children and the natural world. As a sign of respect for this sacred place, the cheerful voices fade away as the children approach the forest. This omnipresent respect for everything that lives there including their ancestors is moving.

Music emerges from the heart of the warm and rich forest. The latter brings an atmosphere of comfort and relaxation allowing all children to obtain a place of rejuvenation or rest. I perceive the unity that connects the children to each other. In small groups of ten, they position themselves in a circle. Between them vibrations are exchanged that manifest themselves in a glittering sphere. The latter lights up the assembly of children. This intense light expands widely and flies away to radiate into the universe. When we are able to connect to it, it is a source of healing from suffering and pain. Luminous insects illuminate the half-light of this space, revealing the silhouettes of some children already asleep further away. By the glow of a fire, others sip on an infused herb from the trees. My attention turns to the right. I note the presence of ancestors from whom an ageless aura emanates. Their energies are displayed in a multitude of extravagant layers of color. I have never seen anything like this phenomenon. One of them sits on a bench near a library overflowing with books from a diverse collection.

I am attracted to some of them, very bright, who keep away from the others. They are thin and radiate a bright white light so intense that I am dazzled. The desire to ask questions, to dialogue with them and to unravel the mysteries of their existence jostles inside me. For the moment, I am content to examine what is unfolding before me.

With unexpected strength a force pulls me in the direction of the St. Lawrence River superimposed on the location in which I find myself. An electrifying energy connects the City to the water below. Complex shapes that resemble coded writing are drawn all along this thread towards the City. By touching it, its brightness and vibrations increase. I decide to reach out to the current. Instantly, an induction runs through me. A torch of light bursts. The connection with this energy is not unknown to me. A sudden, burning, paralyzing pain penetrates the walls of my head, as if a blow had been received shattering my skull... I see a fragment of my soul split open into the universe around me. Second by second, segments of memories from the age of five resurface. I find myself catapulted a decade back. I remember walking towards a luminous bridge leading to a dome shape: this is the City of Light. My body hurts, especially my head. Surprisingly, without doing anything, the pain dissipates with each step taken. The healing energy flows through me. The metamorphosis that is taking place is surprising.

My first meeting

I feel an enveloping presence. The more I advance, the more a lively and flamboyant aura manifests itself. It comes from a really radiant old lady that I can see at the other end. Along the way, I hear the echoes of a mixture of harmonious interactions: bursts of laughter from children playing in the waterfalls, animals frolicking with them or exchanges between the vegetation and the young people. This symphony perfectly illustrates the connection between everything in front of me. All the splendor of life beyond the limits of earthly reality is expressed. Moreover, it's paradise and I'm part of it! The sense of love and harmony, sharing and support takes shape in me as I finish crossing the glittering bridge.

In the vicinity of this sanctuary, I feel totally at ease, safe and connected to all that Is. A sense of belonging encapsulates in me. I huddle in a hollow between two large roots of a towering tree whose foot is lined with moss. Animals of all kinds accompany me. Everything is peaceful. In this space, for the first time, I became aware of the inner movement of the water present in every element: the molecules, the atoms of the human body, the animals, the insects, the trees, the plants, the planet itself. I also hear the sound of every vibration, of every movement, of all that is. The old lady appears directly at my side. Her touch, as delicate as a feather, reassures me. Her presence transmits an extremely powerful energy. Then, a hologram begins to appear before my eyes. I see a snippet of my existence – past, present, future – as well as interstellar and multidimensional travel. This revelation of my unique essence leaves me stunned, but at the same time serene in this new experience. The old lady takes my hand. I am charmed by her reassuring voice that pronounces words that touch me even in my soul:

— "Anick, are you ready to go back to your family? You have been rescued. A team has travelled from far and wide to bring you back here. I have been working in this place for hundreds of years. I will always be with you. You are now safe. You now know how to heal yourself. When you crossed the bridge, it was your energy that was reducing the headache. Now trust in the power of your healing spirit."

I'm rather perplexed. I stay silent as I try to make sense of the situation, the elements of another life begin to unfold. The lady goes on to detail events that join certain fragments of distant memories buried in my mind. Everything is slowly and clearly coming back. In more or less conscious proportions, an inner relief sets in. I discover an answer to the existential questions that have assailed me for so long. I understand that the gift of healing is part of my life mission: my purpose on Earth has been found! Once again, the course of my life changes irrevocably. A new chapter awaits me. On the horizon, a journey towards new perspectives is taking shape.

Delicately, I return to my weak and suffering body which is near the patio behind the house.

Adventure and rescue

Weeks go by and I stay in bed. My body is unable to handle the simplest tasks. My weakness makes me powerless, unable to bring even a spoon to my mouth to feed myself. The holiday season is coming and I'm celebrating Christmas and New Year's Eve from the confines of my bed. On a very cold January morning, I wake up with a frightening realization: I am alone in the house. Every day of the week, my mother accompanies my younger sisters to school and informs me of her departure. On this day, this is not the case. Maybe she wanted to let me sleep and thought she would have time to come back before I woke up?

The idea of the comfort of a hot bath soothes me. Every step feels like an arduous effort, as the pain had taken root in my frail figure. I lean heavily against the wall to stay upright and make my way to the bathroom. I manage to gather the last remainder of strength to pull myself into the bathtub. The warm water embraces me, and a relief gradually spreads through my aching limbs. The value of this temporary respite is priceless. I feel liberated. Time seems to fade in this cocoon of tranquility. I can't accurately gauge how much time I spent immersed in this soothing water. When I get out of the bath, my body is unstable, and dizziness takes hold of me. My balance is shaking. I quickly get confused and hear myself screaming "Mom! Mother!"

This excruciating pain, now familiar, resurfaces in my head again. This time, the intense pulsation pulls me to the ground. In an instant, the energy changes. I feel so good! I'm no longer in my body. It is only an envelope, but my mind is complete. I fly over the room, I see my body lying on the floor and yet, I have no emotion. As I wander around, I feel my body go into a transparent vortex. I go back once again to the age of five. In this episode, my three-year-old sister is sitting in front of me. A sweltering heat permeates the house as we eat breakfast. Tranquility gives way to panic when suddenly, my sister's eyes roll back. Her body begins to convulse in a frightening way (we later learn when she arrives at the hospital that this is the crucial beginning of her diabetes). Fear takes hold of me, and I cry out to my mother for help. As a powerless witness to the unfolding drama, my body becomes rigid and cold. It triggered the dorsal vagal system, having my body immediately shut down because my brain can't handle what it is being dealt with. I feel my spirit beginning to detach from my physical form. I'm standing, right next to my own body. I am pushed further away from my physical form with a distorted virulence. Overwhelmed by despair and tears flowing freely, my mother rushes to my sister's side. From the depths of my being, I scream begging my mother to protect me. This otherworldly grip paralyzes me entirely, taking me further and further. My consciousness vanishes as I am forced to go out against my will.

Hovering in the atmosphere, consumed by panic, I scream my distress. Time is indistinct. I don't know where I am anymore, or who I am. I don't understand where I'm going. This misadventure seems like an eternity to me. At some point, I open my eyes: it's very dark and incredibly warm. I look around and realize that I am in what looks like a van. I am confined in a cage alongside a group of frightened children unsure of the circumstances that have led them to this disorienting interior. This desolate place is unlike anything I have ever experienced. Through the small cracks in the vehicle, I observe the changing movements of day and night. We are locked up in a cramped space, living an ordeal that stretches on endlessly. Communication between us is limited to silent exchanges through our eyes and the occasional tired smile. The abductors have a human appearance, but without presence: a body without a soul, an empty shell without any expression.

An indefinite period passes. My state boils down to rocking, bent into a little ball and humming to myself to get comfort. There are sounds and noises around when a new electric chirping sound starts in my head. This novelty attracts my attention and takes me out of the desolation in which I have been stuck since my arrival in what I presume was a cage. A hidden wisdom (I don't really know in which corner of my being) makes its way into my reasoning. I turn my head to look next to me. Intuition makes me stretch my fingers towards a girl in the neighboring cage. The pain of the rapture is the common point that unites us. I share a melody with her that I create note by note, as I usually do for myself. Our silent connection comforts us in the midst of suffering. Suddenly, the kidnappers return. They brought another young girl back to the cage next to mine in a deteriorated state. I hide my gaze from her captors and look at the girl's eyes filled with tears. I touch her fingers as support. In a brief moment, her eyes change from sorrow to radiant gratitude. Without words, through her eyes, I feel her thanks for the healing contact that took place in her. This simple exchange of energy creates a powerful effect. This is what makes me aware of a new capacity within me: I emit, from the sounds in my head, a magnetism that allows me to create a protective barrier. This transparent shell resembles a bubble displaying the color spectrum. This light shield serves as a natural protection on command. Initiated by the gesture of reaching out, a transformation is triggered. A chain reaction of emotions and connections spreads to each of us. I start exhibiting to the other kids how to harness this innate power that they have as well. Connected to each other by our fingers for days and days, we create a common protective web. I guide them in the art of making their own transparent shell. Whenever a child is chosen for their duty of captivity, the rest of us connect to a powerful level of consciousness. We are immersed in a high collective vibration that protects us from suffering. These luminous spheres disturb those who subject us to this ordeal, undermining their influence and malevolent control. This new energy that we create is love. This new capacity is a source of resilience. Proof that unity generates strength and makes courage flourish in the most difficult circumstances. Hours, weeks, and months seem to mix up. The concept of time is still elusive, as if we were in non-time.

One day, a change seeps into this energy. The scent is different. It carries an aura of love and kindness. Unexpectedly, the door of the van opens. A group of human and non-human individuals dressed in uniform enter the vehicle. The noise ceases to exist. Their mere presence envelops us in relief and makes us slip into a state of trance. The notion of time is moving again. It is the return of the "eternal present". In an instant, our weakening fades. With impressive efficiency, the team of rescuers unlock our cages and lead all the children back to an immense spaceship. Inside, a world diametrically opposed to the van awaits us: an abundance of food, water and beneficial light. These compassionate Beings guide my friends and I to a place where we are purified and healed. We are then placed in beds surrounded by machines that seem to be living and whose voices have feminine melody. I am relished with this attention and this unconditional love. In my understanding as a child, our time aboard this spaceship is counted in days. I marvel at the strange fate that has led us to darkness and then to a realm whose environment is filled with light.

To allow us to understand, the team of rescuers informs us of the circumstances surrounding our rescue. They explain that the operation took longer than expected. It was in the direction of a group of children subjected to genetic manipulation. The ship veered toward our location when it captured our collective energy that was unfolding from our shield created by the strength of our unit. The bursts of light, love and warmth that emanated from it caught their attention, like a lighthouse in the dark. In the space of a few moments, at least 200 children from various origins and galaxies join us in this safe place. They are deeply wronged by misadventures. Some are still very sick. The spectacle is heartbreaking. We are surrounded by a large rescue team that exudes nothing but love and compassion. The gigantic door of the room opens. A striking-looking woman with long, flowing, blonde-grey hair makes her entrance. I feel like I recognize her. I feel like I've met her before! She greets the team by raising her hand, then turns her gaze to us. With a warm smile, she says welcome into her world. She assures us that there is only tranquility, comfort, and security here in order to heal. Through its presence, the atmosphere of well-being is concretized in each of the particles that compose me, chasing away the last residues of emptiness that were lying around in me. It is now total comfort.

In the distance, I hear my mother's panicked screams reaching my ears. Suddenly, I find myself on the floor next to my hot water bath. Back on Earth, I am disoriented.

⸺ "Anick! Anick! Wake up! What happened?"

Her worried voice makes me realize that, although my experience lasted only a few minutes in human time, I felt like I had spent years in another dimension. As I gradually come back to myself, I forget the event that had just happened in the same way that one leaves a dream when waking up. That same day, a visit to the doctor is planned. The doctor's diagnosis confirmed a very severe mononucleosis that requires complete rest. A few days later, my father's job took him to a store near Indigenous lands. He knows the local population well, including an elder skilled in natural medicine. This wise man recommends exposing myself to the energy of the sun, emphasizing that it is essential to my healing.

A second encounter: rebirth

February marked the start of my sixth month in bed. Every winter, my family travels south for a few weeks to get a rest from the season. My parents decide to go on a trip to Florida in our motorhome. Despite my condition, this year was no exception. During the two-day journey, I am in a constant state of sleep. At the destination, we are allowed to park directly on Daytona Beach. After we have settled in, my father opens the doors and my younger sisters hurriedly get out of the motorhome. Awake, I feel lucky to be close to the sea. The salt air does me so much good. The heat accumulated in the sand invites me to push back the weakness of my body in order to energize myself with the help of the four elements within my reach: water, air, earth and sun. My first steps are slow and unstable when I get out of the RV. One foot at a time, I venture further. A feeling out of the ordinary begins to rise in me. I don't understand where it comes from. I persevere in walking until I reach the water's edge. As soon as my feet are bathed in the sea, a strength springs from within. I feel like I'm being pushed forward. I'm going on a journey to another dimension. It is then that I notice a figure walking next to me. She looks like a future version of myself which, suddenly, reminds me of the old lady who lives in the City of Light. This observation is really intriguing! With a determined voice and a measured tone, she says to me:

— "Hello Anick! Unlike the times before, you will remember all the content of today's meeting."

She holds the key to unlock my mission for the future. Her gaze remains fixed on me. She exudes an aura of calm authority.

— "I spend most of my time in the City of Light for children. You know it as we have shown it to you many times. My primary responsibility is to take care of the young souls when new groups of rescued children arrive. Many of them are severely scarred by painful trauma."

At these words, the veil of protection over this memory is removed. I'm back in my life at five years old. Everything goes by in no time without the emotion of the trauma: my sister's discomfort, my disappearance, the care of the City of Light, and my departure and return to the exact time and space of when I left the scene of the incident in the kitchen with my sister. I still wonder about the nature of my experiences.

How can I leave my body, live elsewhere for what seems like months or years, and re-enter it at the very moment I left? Is life a tangle of mysteries where all our scenarios coexist at the same time?

The ageless old lady goes on to explain her role in more detail:

— "I constantly watch over them and provide them with care 24 hours a day. I don't need rest or sleep. My overflowing energy is supported by codes of light. In addition, they provide enough electricity to power the entire facility."

She goes on to describe the stages of the rescue, as I had experienced them, as well as the necessary coordination between the different teams for the benefit of these little living beings:

⊢ "Our rescuers are both humans and non-humans. That is to say, they have a human appearance by their physical profile. However, the components of their faces look different. I receive telepathic messages about two days in advance, letting us know the number of young people we will host and the circumstances from which they come. My team is exceptionally competent. The members are handpicked. We are carefully preparing for the arrival of the little ones who come from all over the galaxy. The rescue spaceship is directly connected to the healing energy of the City of Light, which is specially designed for all children. As soon as the victims are found and transported, a form of care begins. Their vital cord fragment is regenerated by harmonious vibrations and sounds. We welcome them on a bridge imperceptible to the human eye that is connected to the City of Light. Sometimes I stay in the newly arrived vessel to help souls reintegrate into their damaged physical bodies."

I am impressed by all the details provided. The old lady insists on the importance of time and the high quality of care for children, because they are precious and sacred:

⊢ "The care is done in a comprehensive way, regardless of its various origins," she says. "Once all the children are settled on beds, I transmit a unique energy in code and vibration. Subsequently, a form of electricity modifies their DNA into a more appropriate configuration. I then activate a new custom chip that harmonizes with their new state. These beds are equipped with advanced technological machines. They emit waves, sounds, and colors, linked to a higher intelligence of high frequency. The whole thing looks like Morse code. The Language of the Stars unfolds with my energies."

⊢ "All Beings of Light work together to repair the energies of each child by creating a space for real and lasting healing and transformation. Children from various corners of the galaxy hold the ability to connect to the sound and vibration of love. My role is to help weakened souls integrate into our civilization while they stay with us.

Once their condition improves, they are gradually allowed to venture out of the medical center to explore the City's abundant resources. At this point, collaboration with the Blue Beings and Mantises that live here is essential for the rehabilitation of the survivors. Everyone recovers at their own pace. When the time is right, they emerge free of psychological, physical, and emotional scars. Memories of the trauma tend to fade, leaving behind only a vague sense of discomfort. Only children who volunteer will consciously remember or those who experience déjà vu will have access to it."

— "When a child is deemed ready, the preparation for its return begins. The soul has two choices. The first is to join their family. The transition is smooth. Each little being is reinserted unnoticed into their physical body. They return to the exact place, to the same date, to the precise time and to the second that they left during their trauma. The second is to stay with us in the City. When the soul chooses to stay, it has two options: either to leave the body permanently (physical death), or a fragment of the soul re-enters the body and continues its life. The impact of trauma creates an infinite amount of soul divisions. One of these divisions chooses to settle in the body that remains in the plane where the trauma occurs."

These revelations leave me speechless. It's a truly grim fate that no child should have to endure. I keep telling myself that all trauma is the result of a plan that we selected before we came to life on Earth. In return, a profound transformation takes place. Special abilities and gifts occur.

The many questions that simmer about the meaning of my adventures are answered. Am I the only one who remembers such events? Probably not! Have others around me experienced similar situations? Where are they? Was my sister kidnapped when she was seriously ill in the kitchen, too? The idea of meeting other people who share an experience like mine leaves me curious and excited.

Always confident, with a solemn tone, the wise lady demystifies the reason for child abductions.

— "Children who experience intense shocks have a natural ability to get out of their bodies as a protective mechanism. At this moment, their soul is delicately held in place by a fragile strand at the navel button. This wire is severed when the child is abducted. It is therefore relatively easy for negative entities to capture the souls of children in distress. The risks that are involved are serious for them. Stolen in this way, they are subjected to scientific experimentation, trafficking, genetic cloning, and manipulation of their DNA."

Throughout her speech, a sincere love and a lively commitment are palpable. The firm tone of her words underlines the crucial importance of the rescue mission she is leading, accompanied by her entire team. As with every encounter with this woman, her presence of unconditional love envelops me. This time, she gently merges body to body with me. My weakened version evaporates. Then suddenly, a fragment of my soul "of a new self" immediately enters my body. It's like receiving a complete update from the inside out. Once again, the limits of time are suspended: a few hours seemed like a few minutes. As this metamorphosis occurs, I realize that this extraordinary woman, who visited me, is none other than a future version of myself. One of my higher selves. My mission is clearly confirmed: to help the children of the universe here on Earth in the wonderful City of Light. This affirmation is divinely well harmonized with the essence of my being.

Back in my body, both feet in the ocean, I continue my journey along the beach with confident steps. Transformed, I feel my stature upright and vitalized. The words that come to my ears bring me back to an in-between of the two worlds. I'm a little out of step with reality. I hear two girls next to me talking to two adults who are looking at me and whom they call "Daddy, Mommy". The woman says:

— "Come on, we're leaving! Anick, come on!"

Slowly, my memory readjusts, and it will be once I am installed in the motorhome that I recognize that these people are members of my family. In the astonished eyes of my parents, you can read the total incomprehension of the unexpected change they are witnessing. I was more than weak and constantly bedridden just a while ago. Although they can't fully grasp how this change had happened, my father and mother are simply thrilled to see my improved health and renewed drive. Just breathing in the clean ocean air and basking in the sun's regenerative energy helped to do wonders. My new personality, that is, the new version of myself, is much more mature.

In the weeks that followed, my grandfather reappeared and ended his prolonged absence. His return is almost a coincidence. The reflection that everything has been orchestrated comes back in a loop, as if the universe is conspiring to compassionately guide me through my evolutionary path. This is the beginning of another new chapter of rebirth, renewal, and emergence in my life.

Chapter 6

The message from this Lady

The lady, who is my guide and my source of knowledge, visits me several times during adolescence until the age of 25. The repercussions of her ideas and messages have a major impact on me. The implications of the revelations upset me. Here is a message that has been coming true for at least two decades and that still resonates with my conscience and the observation of my current life:

— More and more children of the new Earth are incarnating with an energy that is nothing short of supernatural. Their vibration of unconditional love extends throughout the immense universe. However, their higher potential is triggered as a result of a shock or an accumulation of these through the many lives of their soul. First of all, we must remember that on Earth, the brain's ability to put things into perspective is established around the age of twelve. Before this age, the emotions experienced are impregnated in their raw state, without filter and without reasoning in the nervous system. Many situations act as a trauma: difficult birth, neonatal distress, separation or abandonment, violent environment, violence or abuse, serious illness, or the introduction of certain substances such as vaccines, regardless of the virus linked to them. These elements can inadvertently cause their souls to detach from their human vessels. These distressed souls are vulnerable to being seized by low-frequency entities. In a matter of hours, minutes or even seconds, their essence can be lost. These children's souls can become fragmented, lost and often could become candidates for various uses: teleportation to other realities, manipulation of time and space or for remote viewing and even espionage. A part of themselves is trapped in the dark side of multidimensionality. A soul division, shard fragment could be held captive in underground facilities, such as the cities hidden in the hollows of the mountains or even in another cosmos, or universe. These places are usually inaccessible to ordinary individuals. Some access can be through portals at the North and South Poles or inside the enigmatic Bermuda Triangle. In these mysterious places, I can see the spirits of the children. They are connected to a malevolent intelligent force that feeds on their energy. Hypnotized, they are manipulated and used continuously, 24 hours a day. Being caught up in both a world of misuse and our earthly realm, these children cannot function normally. As a result, they disconnect from their human bodies. They therefore need to be supervised and guided.

It is becoming obvious that, in our societies, these remarkable and ultra-bright children are labelled as people with neurodevelopmental disorders such as autism, Asperger's syndrome and/or sensory impairments. Repetitive and limiting behaviors are proportionally related to the manipulations imposed on them as victims. As a result, they adopt different coping mechanisms: rigidity, flapping, withdrawal, having restricted interests, obsessions with certain objects or themes, difficulties with social skills, difficult or absent verbal communication. These children try to maintain a balance between two completely opposite and complex realities in which they are entangled in. Society has always tried to form atypical people to the functioning of the masses. Given the rather mixed results, current norms and standards are being questioned more seriously. Slowly, but surely, openness is becoming more present. It allows for better understanding and therefore more effective interactions will result. The same is true for other diagnoses. For example, syndromes with intellectual and visual disabilities that are not able to be autonomous in our system.

The scale and scope of these revelations changed my perception of the challenges of these exceptional children. They need help to recover their spirit, as it is fragmented. It is essential to reintegrate them into our world. These geniuses of our time are divided into new existences. This offers them the opportunity to be saved just as I was. When we perceive signs of evolution in their development, it is because a different communication, other than verbal, has taken place at the level of the soul.

Energetically, a change has taken place. The disclosure of this information indicates that the language used in our society is intentionally manipulated. By inducing false beliefs, humans become limited.

As soon as they are transported to the City of Light, the children live parallel lives different from those from which they were freed. The rehabilitation time is specific to each person. Sometimes it's throughout their entire present lives.

During the day, they live on the earth plane. Their presence stimulates people's awakening and teaches to be oneself among the values advocated by their performance system. Let's remember that these extraordinary young people have chosen their families beforehand!

The traumas they experienced catalyze the activation of their DNA in a specific way. At night, all the children who have been saved and those whose part of the soul is still fragmented exist in the City of Light. The survivors get there by teleporting. It is in this realm that they are aware of their abilities. They discuss their mission roles using the Language of the Stars. They help maintain the energetic balance of the different components of humanity. Their support extends to Earthlings, animals, natural elements (water, air, earth, fire, ether), warriors of light and the cosmos. These are just a few examples of their fields of action.

Their giftedness in specific areas (which are sometimes treated as obsessions) is a misunderstood testimony to their function in the other lives they live. This information was given to me a very long time ago. When memories of my abduction at age five resurfaced—through my implicit memory--I knew I was being chosen to share what some children are going through right now. It's part of a contract that we accepted before we incarnated.

Chapter 7

Discovering the World

As the years go by and I get closer to the adult world, a multitude of questions continue to swirl around inside me. On the morning of my eighteenth birthday, my mind is buzzing. What kind of work do I want to do? How can I actualize the true call that whispers in the depths of my being? I know what my life mission is and my role in this wide world. Should I accomplish my goal now or can I enjoy the freedom that youth offers without the seriousness of responsibility? The answers remain uncertain. However, one desire abounds in the midst of hesitation: to leave Quebec. This place reminds me of too many things from the past. I aspire to adventure, to a chance to redefine my identity and discover unexplored territories. Internally, I need a big change of scenery.

In the summer, I work as a counsellor at a youth camp. I love this role! I find comfort in being with children. Those who carry within them loneliness, sadness, abandonment, or distress call on me. My heart swells with compassion and I devote all my attention to them in renewed energy. That year, a golden opportunity presented itself at the camp: an exchange program with a group of counsellors in France, in the beautiful French Alps. This camp is for teens struggling with childhood trauma. It's an offer that immediately appeals to me. In addition, skiing is a passion that has always held a special place in my heart. Fate perfectly orchestrates my desires, my talents, my passion, and the possibility of getting out of Quebec! Just thinking about it makes my heart race. I feel my wings spread to take flight towards a new world that awaits me with open arms. The day I find out I've been selected is a moment of pure euphoria. It's a perfect job for me!

France

A few weeks later, I find myself on an airplane bound for St-Jean-de-Maurienne, a charming town in the Maurienne Valley of the French Alps located southeast of Mont Blanc. The beauty is breathtaking. With unwavering determination, I know that this is where I am meant to be.

When I arrive, friendly instructors welcome me. Each one is a shining star in its own right. A beautiful synergy emerges. It is in this enchanting setting that my vocation is confirmed. This experience validates my ability to not only provide authentic help, but also transform the lives of these teens. I rediscover an ability that sets me apart from others during my time at camp. I interact with the ancestorial spirits of the teenagers in my group, just as I could with my own grandfather. This gift allows me to learn more about the struggles and issues that occupy these young souls. By connecting to the energy of their ancestors, I bridge the gap between the world of the deceased and the present moment. Through this connection, I receive considerable information and knowledge. I gain wisdom that guides me in my mission to comfort and heal their descendants. These lessons keep me modest about them. With each interaction, I realize the privilege I have. The radiant smiles that replace the painful expressions bring me beautiful happiness. My work is a source of immense joy. Of course, I have my secret about my invisible work tools. I know that my colleagues at this time do not understand my connection to the spiritual world. There is a fear around this subject. I regularly wonder why society does not accept these natural gifts. It seems to me that if schools taught the invisible, demystified it and taught us how to coexist with it, life would be so much easier for everyone. It would be that simple!

Nevertheless, my colleagues have noticed that I am comfortable building a relationship of trust with the teens and those around me. The sense of well-being I bring to the camp is undeniable. Even though they probably don't understand the mystical aspects of my work, they recognize the real impact of it. Three times a week, I give ski lessons as a camp instructor. I feel at home in the Alps. However, I didn't know this place before I set foot there. Once again, it is in the heart of Mother Nature that my new sanctuary of comfort is composed: the presence of trees, the pristine white of snow, and the embrace of the sun. This enchanting setting feeds the bond of belonging and the telepathic dialogue with all the elements around me.

One day, while waiting for the teens under the gentle caress of the sun, I take a moment to rest. I put my skis in an X shape to signify my presence on the side of the slope and I take a seat on a massive rock bare of its snow. I close my eyes and let the sun's rays flood my face. The serenity of the moment is beneficial. As I open my eyelids, I see something unexpected in the sky. An indistinct shape gradually emerges in the middle of the clouds. I blink repeatedly. With my heart pounding, I close my eyelids and this time I connect my consciousness to the form. I open them again and voila! It is here, the incredible City of Light! Ecstasy fills me and tears come falling down as I contemplate it. A divine presence follows me! This reunion warmly gladdens my heart. I wish to never leave this exciting moment. However, like a fleeting dream, it disappears in the blink of an eye, leaving me wanting more. Week after week, month after month, I try to reconnect with the City of Light, which remains elusive. Despite my nostalgia, I am grateful to have been able to live for nearly six months in the splendor of the French Alps, spend time with exceptional teammates, meet the ancestors of the children I helped and make beautiful discoveries about myself. I leave the French mountains with a bit of sadness.

Return to Canada

I have made the decision to embark on a new adventure that will take me to the towering Rockies of Western Canada. It's hard for me to resist the lure of the mountains, the beauty of the wilderness and the abundance of forests and wildlife. It's the perfect opportunity to take on a challenge: to immerse myself in the English language, since I'm not very skilled at it. The heart and mind of the adventurer that I am are served once I arrive at my destination. This new phase of my life begins with the illustrious Fairmont hotels. These are renowned establishments that have been attracting tourists since the days of the construction of the railroad in the late 1800's. That summer, I also worked for the Rocky Mountain Railway, a local touristic railroad company.

The atmosphere buzzes with excitement as the train prepares to leave. I oversee a section of the train that has a group of enthusiastic customers that day. I explain emergency protocols to passengers and prepare my cart to serve breakfast. I'm absorbed in my tasks when a bizarre encounter disrupts my routine. A young woman wearing a long dress sweeping the floor, appears next to me. She says politely:

— "Excuse me, ma'am, there's someone in my seat."

She stretches out her arm to show her ticket. This gesture disturbs me for a fraction of a second. This train does not require a physical ticket. Her request is sincere. After a quick visual check, the designated seat was claimed by another passenger. The disbelief increases when I turn back to the lady, and I see that these clothes belong in another era: that of the early 1900s. It is then that everything became clear. I can't believe I'm being disrupted in the middle of work by a spirit! With a touch of impatience, I inform her that I don't have time at the moment. In fact, I am more concerned about the needs of my group. The lady soon disappears from my field of vision. Many times, over time, I meet deceased people who come forward without warning, out of curiosity or a desire for attention. I order them to appear only when I am unoccupied, knowing that they have no notion of time. This brief moment passes, and the demands of the guests occupy my attention again. I can't resist the urge to briefly look in her direction to check her presence or to try to determine the exact year she came from. A few hours later, in a rare moment of respite, I intend to go and apologize for my behavior. Unfortunately, when the train stops, the lady or rather the ghost had disappeared. The missed opportunity weighs on me and regret arises. Her intriguing presence will remain engraved in my memory.

The following winter took me into the hectic world of hospitality. My first year was marked by a particularly chilling encounter at the Jasper Park Lodge Hotel. In the evening, I have the task of dropping off a bottle of Port in one of the villas for a client who is about to register his stay. The villa in question is located in the forest a short distance from the main building of the hotel. The villa has quite a reputation among my colleagues. They occasionally tell frightening stories about their encounters. Strange demonstrations have taken place in many of those cabins. So, I admit that the prospect of venturing there alone makes me a little anxious. This is a surprising irony since I am, after all, an expert in the field of the paranormal. With the desire to impress my boss and warmly welcome the prestigious guests, I put aside my mistrust. I leave to make my delivery. That evening, a fierce snowstorm raged outside.

The mercury indicates a temperature below 30 degrees Celsius. The closer I get to the villa, the heavier the atmosphere is. An eerie silence sends shivers throughout my body. I unlock the door and enter the dimly lit hallway. I immediately take off my big white boots clumped with snow. For ease of safely handling my delicate items, I take off my coat. I head to a room with a huge fireplace. Next to it stands an abundant pile of dry wood. The fire will be prepared by a colleague delegated to this task. I carefully place the bottle and glasses on the small table in front. Suddenly, a visit of a spectral nature is felt. My gaze turns to the fireplace. Without explanation, flames broke out in the fireplace! The fire dances calmly. Background music is suddenly added. When I turn around, I see a woman sitting on the sofa. Her clothing dates from the 1920s. Panic takes hold of me. Without a second thought, I rush to the door without picking up my coat and my dripping boots on the entrance carpet. Outside, the icy air pierces my skin, but I'm too scared to realize it. After a few minutes, I realize that I came out with nothing. A burst of lucidity dislodges the fear that pulsates within me. I return to the villa. Wondering why I fled so quickly, I open the door, put on my boots, and wrap myself in my coat. After reflection, I realize that what pushed me to flee was the influence of my colleagues with their stories of supernatural occurrences. Coming to my senses, this encounter affects me because of the deep sadness that emanates from the woman. Staff members have already mentioned that her presence is a recurring occurrence in this place. She is frequently seen sitting near a window. Accounts report hearing her saddened cry. Apparently, she is waiting in the hope that a certain lover will join her. From this unfulfilled love, despair led her to a tragic end; She is said to have committed suicide. It's no wonder the staff are hesitant to enter this place in the evening. The next day, I plucked up the courage to return to the villa. I hope to meet the spirit of the young woman, but nothing happens. This scene, although unnerving, is another testimony of the paranormal world that intertwines with the reality I have chosen to embrace.

Without naming them all, working at ancient hotels like Jasper Park Lodge and the Banff Springs Hotel has opened my eyes to many other supernatural events. The establishments have rich histories. The spirits of the past seem to linger, trapped between the world of the living and the dead. Over time and with the accumulation of experiences, I realize that these apparitions are not malicious. These confused and lost deceased are simply reacting to our fear and distress. By gently letting them know that they are rather in another century, it allows them to understand their situation and find their way to the afterlife. Through this learning, I realize the importance of compassion and help, even for those who live in the ethereal world.

When fall arrives, I'm back in Quebec. However, this is only a brief stopover on my journey to other destinations.

Taiwan

My thirst to travel, explore and understand the world is still strong. I can't wait to continue, as I take the opportunity to go and work in Asia. The diversity of cultures and the richness of their histories attract me. My choice is Taiwan, more precisely a village outside of Taoyuan. I teach English and French to children. Once again, I have the privilege of being in contact with the ancestors of the people I meet. I develop an affinity with certain spirits that protect me on this sacred island. We make an agreement: I promise to protect the children here and to teach them. In return, they have to protect me and notify me by a sign when I have to leave for something else. My path is intertwined with the company of ancestral spirits, no matter where I venture in the world.

My stay at Kenting National Park, located on a beach in southern Taiwan, becomes a pivotal moment. One weekend evening, on an excursion with friends, I experienced a moment of pure ecstasy. On the sandy shores, I am pampered by the presence of the ocean and the murmur of its breeze. The soft light of the moon creates a vaporous atmosphere. As the night progresses, I find myself alone on the beach, with only a tourist map of the world in my hand. It is precisely one o'clock in the morning. In my moment of reflection, I look for answers about the path my life will take for the future. For a year and a half, Taiwan was my home. It is a place of revelations and transformations. The moment I look at the map to find where I will go, the universe reacts with a sign. The sky turns into a fantastic show of lights. Shocked and speechless, I witness the arrival of a huge otherworldly structure. In this stunning moment, I whisper: "Thank you for showing me this hidden treasure!"

Before my eyes, the City of Light materializes. Its luminosity sketches a blue aura that blends perfectly with the atmosphere. The distant sound of a celestial symphony caresses my ears. I feel like I'm in communion with life itself. I now understand the meaning and purpose of what I was trying to achieve in this country. I understand that I am always in the right place, at the right time, guided by a celestial star that lights the way to my next adventure. From there, my intuition guides me to Japan. Fabulous discoveries about the greatness of the being that I am await me.

Japan

Japan welcomes me. I settle in a charming village of Kagoshima, located in the southwest of the country. It's a place with an amazing energy. The volcanic landscape that surrounds whispers ancient tales of the Earth's power. My journey took me to the impressive Ebino Plateau and the magnificent Mount Karakuni, both shrouded in the presence of sulfur. I join my friend Emi, whom I met when I worked at the Fairmont Jasper Park Lodge. We have forged a bond that resists past borders, time, and distance. As we reach Mount Karakuni near my friend's house, an unforeseen encounter takes place. A man dressed in an outfit resembling dark kimono pajamas approaches me. He has a very enthusiastic air of gratitude. Oddly enough, my understanding of the Japanese language is effortless. I answer him telepathically:

— "What are you talking about? I've never been here in my life."

The man looks at me contemplatively. The words he strings together leave me completely stunned.

⊢ "But yes, you are a great lady," he continues.

⊢ "You protect the women and children of the village, you have absolute respect from all of us, but I understand that you are very humble."

The hesitation continues during the analysis of the words of this stranger. I am beginning to doubt the veracity of what I am experiencing. I feel like I'm in a dream. I glance around. I then realize that I have transported myself into the unfolding of a past life. The man stands in front of the Mount Karakuni volcano. I see myself as a woman draped in a kimono. I'm a warrior. My hands grip long war knives. The scene unfolds vehemently. I don't fully understand the meaning of this vision. I also do not wish to fully grasp the implications because a feeling of discomfort persists. All the while, my friend and her husband are standing by my side. Their presence offers me both comfort and a sense of rootedness. The messenger from the distant past explains to me that he has known me for a very long time. He considers me a valuable member of his army. He assures me that I will always be protected in his country by his ancestors. Their watchful spirits surround me in the present, as they have done through the ages. Before he leaves, the dark man informs me that he will soon incarnate to keep the connection alive. I am convinced that this man is embodied in the son of my friend who was with me during my trip. Since that time, I have not seen them again. Neither the son, nor the old man, but Emi and I continue to develop a beautiful friendship.

Each new country I visit seems to serve as a portal to a realm of positive and / or negative energies. It's like I'm reliving the emotions of other lives. In my quest, by absorbing the essence of each place, I unravel the layers of my own identity. I am freeing myself from old burdens. Space is created for new perspectives and to continue my personal growth.

Everything follows one another, nothing is a coincidence

My return to Quebec, Canada leads to an obvious drop in my energy level. I feel a disconnection is growing day by day from the vibrant and enriching experiences that I had through my travels. The contrast is striking, and I am afraid of falling ill. I am reconnecting with my family, of course, but I am destined to return to Western Canada for good. I get a full-time teaching position in an English Montessori school. I pass on the beauty of the French language to children aged five to seven. This role is accompanied by another type of management in parallel. Some toddlers carry inner distress within them. Their anxiety, depression or feeling of helplessness pours into my consciousness. Inevitably, I discern the source of their emotional turmoil. I also see the colors of their energy. The latter allows me to connect with the origins of their repressed negativity. My intuitive gifts have also extended to their parents, as I pick up on the vibrations of the close bond between them. In their pure innocence, children willingly absorb their parents' emotional charges to protect them. This dynamic strikes a chord with me. It's terribly difficult to distance myself from the intensity that constantly swirls around me. It's official, teaching is not a long-term job for me. Although this is an area where I excel, and I am adored by children. Moreover, A different destiny, more aligned with my intuitive skills, is calling me.

In the middle of my teaching career, I find a job at the renowned Fairmont Empress hotel in Victoria Canada. Many paranormal occurrences happen at that hotel. Then I moved to Calgary Canada to go work at the Fairmont Palliser, to continue my journey. All the hotel jobs allow me to interact with a wide range of people and understand their history of the past. At 33 years of age, the search for a remarkable partner who will truly touch my heart remains active. My journey is marked by a series of unsatisfying adventures in the field of love. During my stay in Taiwan, I made a very special request to the ancestors: to send a man into my life that corresponds with my energy. I had described this ideal partner in great detail, listing all the criteria he should possess. It's a sincere vindication of my belief in the power of intention and connection. I learned to write and visualize what I want to manifest, thanks to my grandfather. Thank you for this invaluable teaching! My wish is granted quickly. I soon meet this exceptional man through his sister who is not only a colleague, but also a friend at the hotel where I work. From the first few seconds of feeling his energy, an unshakeable certainty was born and spread deep within me. This intuition confirms to me that this gentleman is for me. It is a soul-to-soul connection, a vibration that logic cannot explain. I see and feel his energy as if he had always been an integral part of my life. Shortly after, I notice my grandfather who's always near me standing with a man at his side. Later, I learn that he is my husband's grandfather. Despite this powerful feeling, I am cautious. I keep the secret of my abilities to myself, afraid of scaring him away with my peculiarities. I wait at least a year before revealing more about this facet of myself.

Chapter 8

Building my nest

Time passes and our relationship deepens. Slowly and surely, I open up to him about some aspects of my extraordinary abilities. Surprisingly, he doesn't flinch or run away in terror! How shocking! This discovery fills me with gratitude and admiration. To my great astonishment, he confides in me elements arising from his Greek heritage and his mother's openness to facts similar to mine. She also speaks of life on other planets and describes vivid dreams that cross the limits of our earthly reality. This similarity further solidifies the bond we share and makes our journey together nothing short of extraordinary.

The day I met his mother in Ecuador was a moment of indefinable connection. I have the distinct impression that I have already known her in another life. Familiarity facilitates our conversations. She reveals something implausible to me: her belief of her origins on the moon Ganymede. Surprising at first, these words resonate pleasantly with me. As I research, I dive into the details of Galileo's first astronomical discovery. Ganymede, orbiting Jupiter, is the largest moon in the entire solar system with its diameter of nearly 5,200 kilometers. It is the only moon to have a magnetosphere[2] and the density of its air is thinner and less dense than here.

I am convinced that the presence of my mother-in-law in my life is a deliberate crossroad. It feels like a reunion that extends beyond our current life. It opens a door to a world that intrigues me greatly. Ganymede and my mother-in-law's connection to the planet draws me in, leading me to believe that I, too, am venturing into other realms without remembering them, consciously. Through it all, one thing

---

[2] The area surrounding a celestial object where its electromagnetic field is located

remains unchanged: my spouse seems thrilled to have met a beloved witch.

The coming of our children

Life is an exciting journey filled with adventures and unforgettable moments with my partner. We travel to several remote places, creating memories that last a lifetime. Two years into our relationship, we get married, reinforcing our commitment to each other. We chose a seven-day fairy-tale cruise in the Eastern Caribbean. This day, filled with love and joy, is spent surrounded by friends and family. My work continues, even though we are on vacation. The exclusive energy in the middle of the ocean leaves me little rest. That night, the wind and sea spoke to me like a long-lost friend. I feel reprogrammed: the knowledge that is acquired at this moment allows a regeneration of my higher Self.

Shortly after our wedding, we decide to adopt a beautiful Golden Retriever dog named Baileys. Her loyalty is touching, and her company is pleasant. Baileys has a way of teaching us the importance of balance and living in the moment. Her boundless energy and unconditional love bring a sense of peace and happiness to our home.

There follows a moment of bliss: I discover that I am pregnant. I'm delighted! However, the anticipation of becoming a mother is both exciting... and doubly distressing when we learn that I am carrying twins. I gladly accept all the support and comfort my husband and Baileys offer me. That year I turned 36, my life will never be the same again. The day I've been looking forward to has arrived. I give birth prematurely to two beautiful babies, a boy and a girl. An extraordinary connection with them occurs from the moment they enter the world. It's as if I've known them forever. Their faces, more precisely their eyes, radiate a déjà vu that is difficult to explain. Have their souls and my soul been connected for a long time? To tell the truth, this bond did not begin with their birth. It was already present during their gestation. A pregnancy is full of surprises, and I know the exact moment it started.

A privileged and protected connection

One night, as I lay in bed, an intriguing event unfolds in front of me. Through my eyelids, an intense, warm flash fills the room. Surprised, I open my eyes. Something delicate and subtle gently settles on my belly. A vague form gradually becomes more vivid and precise. I assume first of all that it is my father's father, who died the week before, who is coming to say goodbye. This is not the case. I instantly perceive six non-human figures surrounding me. They appear as large balls radiating white light. Despite the strangeness of the situation, I am immersed in a calm state. My mind wants to signal panic, but no fear invades me. I feel rather soothed by the energy emanating from these luminous Beings. The message I get is one of comfort, assuring me that everything will be okay. This moment is not the only one that I can describe as unusual during my pregnancy.

Protecting my nest

Five months pregnant, I am woken up from sleep by an increasingly loud noise similar to an approaching train. The walls of our house and the ground shake. Fear makes my heart palpitate: something unusual is happening. I wake up my husband:

— "It's the sound of a train," I whisper with a trembling voice. "I feel the house vibrating! I can't go back to sleep. I have to go and see what's going on." I'm convinced that there's something weird above our house.

My husband, foggy by sleep, senses the urgency in my voice. With a nod, he gets up and we venture outside into the cold night. The strange vibration persists. However, there is nothing in sight. The source of the phenomenon is invisible and remains unexplained. We stand in the darkness, scanning the sky. There is frankly nothing to see. The feeling of something hovering over our house gives us chills. The strangeness of all of this is uncomfortable. After about ten minutes of waiting, a helicopter appears above our house. We can't identify its color, but the sound of its blades cutting through the air doesn't lie about the type of vehicle present. It is suspended at a surprisingly low altitude. This inexplicable presence accentuates my discomfort. I decide to retreat to the safety of our home where I hope to protect myself from everything that is happening outside. This anomaly without rational explanation continues to occur throughout my pregnancy. The strange noises and the almost invisible helicopters continued to appear until after I gave birth, always at the same time, around three in the morning.

And it continues

My stay in the hospital lasts for a week. Meanwhile, the mysterious patrols cease temporarily. In my little bed in the birth room, elated to be a mother, I contemplate my beautiful newborns. The outside world takes a back seat in my reality. This moment is only a brief respite. My questions about the air visits are once again worrying me. I know that they will come back without being able to logically explain the reasons. Delighted to be back home with my twins, the atmosphere is still strewn with a certain worry. Every time I get up to feed them or check on their well-being, the thought of something happening to them during the night, haunts me. My heart pounds as I anticipate the familiar hum of helicopters. I wonder if the strange noises that torment us disturb their sleep. It's as if the vibrations are alerting some kind of authorities coming from something much bigger. Yet, when I enter their room, their wide eyes meet mine. Their innocence and curiosity shine in the soft light.

Visitors from elsewhere follow one another

What captivates me is the daily transformation of my children. I notice that their eyes are different: awakened both to the world here and to a mysterious elsewhere. Their eyes are filled with deep wonder, discovering the Earth for the very first time. Or maybe their one hundredth time. I let them sleep beside each other because it seems to give them a sense of security.

Around the age of two or three months, I begin to hear them chirping with Beings I can neither see nor distinguish. This disturbs me because I usually see these energies. Every time this happens, both of my babies are staring at the same place. It's like they are chatting together with another entity or entities. My infants' voices produce sounds and babble that are only heard later in the development of language. When I hear them talking, I am worried and wonder if they are protected, guided, or even monitored. In these moments, I receive comforting advice from my guides that remind me not to worry. Everything is as it should be. I look at my twins with admiration: their gestures and expressions clearly indicate that they are engaged in some form of communication with unseen entities. These unusual events persisted for about two years. Fortunately, this is not an everyday phenomenon.

As the nights go by, I am often woken up from my sleep by the presence of an otherworldly light. I open my eyes to see it disappear in a fraction of a second. With my eyes closed, I can still feel its presence. This brief meeting lasts only a few minutes. However, my mind is bogged down in doubt. At the same time, a sense of serenity surrounds me, and I am soon bathed in an energy of pure love. It's a feeling that I do not want to ever end. Even if this pure happiness stops, it is a recurring experience that I welcome with open arms. Regularly, I have the irresistible desire to join my children as I feel that they are receiving the same connection, however I prefer that the connection persists without waking them up.

Children and knowledge

I am fortunate to be able to stay at home, to offer close supervision and a stimulating environment filled with love to our children. We opt for multilingualism in the education of our children. With them, I only speak French, my husband only Spanish and together, we converse in English. This linguistic richness is a cultural gift that we offer them.

Year after year, it has become more and more apparent that our children possess skills and ideas that are beyond their young age. When my daughter is only two and a half years old, I often catch her looking at the streetlights outside. At the same time, her hands make skillful and precise movements. It leaves me speechless. At first, I justify this behavior as a simple game with imaginary friends. One day, I find her sitting in front of the window, fascinated by the glow of the streetlights. Curious, I ask her what she is doing. Her answer leaves me stunned:

— "I'm talking to them," she says with confidence.

— "Oh, yes? To whom?" I reply.

— "The lights on the street." She nods.

— "What are they saying?" I question.

— "I'm trying to understand. I don't understand. They are all talking at the same time!" she grunts in frustration.

She then makes sudden movements with her hands.

⊢ "One at a time, ok? You guys are all talking at the same time! Stop doing that!"

⊢I respond, "What language are they speaking? Or how are they communicating with you?"

⊢ "I can't tell you right now. They all talk together. If you talk to me, I can't understand. They transmit information to me through an electricity exchange. It is essential that I understand them."

At 30 months, it is usually impossible to receive and formulate this kind of information. I then understand the importance of allowing her to explore and learn in complete freedom. So, I keep a close eye on her with a mixture of curiosity. My daughter also has the habit of placing herself in front of me when we meet new people. I conclude that it is a way to protect me from their energies. Her intuitive nature is something I value, as it is clear that she possesses an increased perception of the energies of the world around her.

My son, as well, has incredible encounters. When he was about three or four years old, he told us about a dark-skinned man who visited him in his room. This spectral visitor floats in the air. The man sits on the edge of his bed and teaches him mathematics in a way that is totally different from conventional methods. He shows my son numbers, each associated with a distinct color, shape, and vibration that emits a sound attributed to them. With his childlike innocence, he also often says to me:

⊢ "Mom, I can tell if people are from here or another galaxy!"

In response, I reassure him that he must always feel safe, because the Earth is not exclusively inhabited by humans. There are many others who live in different galaxies and come to visit us because they are curious. At the age of six, he revealed another extraordinary gift. He sees numbers spinning around his head when his teacher asks him math questions. The number that stops in front of him corresponds to the answer, which allows him to consistently provide the right solution. I'm amazed by this talent, but not totally surprised. While acknowledging his character, I suspect that this passion is indirectly nourished by his paternal role model, who is an expert in finance.

Every time our children share their feelings or see energies by their side, I insist on the fact that there is no reason to be afraid. I encourage them to ask the Beings to stay or leave, depending on what they wish. I suggest that they communicate with them in silence. I want them to understand that these encounters are only for them, like invisible friends. Between brother and sister, or with friends who have similar abilities, these situations can be shared openly. My goal is to spare them the feelings of isolation and misunderstanding that I experienced during my own childhood. From a young age, I made it a point to teach them a multitude of valuable lessons. I insisted on the importance of connecting with nature. Spending a lot of time outdoors in all temperatures, as well as talking or singing with animals and insects to invigorate the spirit. My commitment to these principles has, on many occasions, set me apart from other parents. This alliance with nature and the world around us is part of our way of life.

Chapter 9

Our sabbatical year of discovery

One afternoon, when my children came home from school, I noticed that they were surprisingly calm. It is my daughter who finally breaks the silence. In a hesitant voice, she begins:

— "Mom, I have friends at school."

— "Yes, I know you have friends at school, sweetie." I guess she's talking about her classmates. The rest of her words catch me off guard:

— "Friends who are not from here mom..."

— "Are they kids like you?"

— "Yes and no."

— "Are there any adults like me among your friends?"

With a nod, she says:

— "There are adults like you, mom. Tall gentlemen sometime come. In fact, they came today. They are nice! They told me to be very careful because I'm losing my abilities."

Worried, I ask her:

— "What do you mean, you're losing your abilities? You will always have your abilities," I tell her to try to reassure her.

She shakes her head, her voice filled with sadness and resignation:

— "No, Mom, they told me they can't talk to me like they used to."

The unease in her words weighs down the atmosphere. With a heavy heart for her, I try to understand why. She adds:

— "It's because of school and the way we learn. They tell me it's not good for us."

The revelation disturbs me deeply. I need guidance. I seek comfort in my connection with my guides and my grandfather whom I have not seen since the birth of my children. The luminous Beings who support me and offer me the specifications are the ones I need here and now. There are two main issues at play. First, the traditional and rigid style of education they receive suppresses their natural abilities. The strict structure and numerous regulations stifle their creativity and curiosity. Second, the constant exposure of teaching through technological devices interferes with the development of their young minds. When my husband comes home at the end of his workday, I tell him about our daughter's revelations. Together, we are deliberating on possible solutions. We recognize the need for change. The next morning, my husband makes an unexpected announcement that delights me:

— "I'm tired right now. I need a break from work. I'm taking a sabbatical."

Immediately, I exclaimed:

— "Really? That's great!"

— "I feel like I really need it. Children need to change schools and the perfect time to do so is now. Let's travel with them!"

I accept without reluctance, excited at the idea of embarking on this new family adventure. It's a fantastic idea! As my enthusiasm skyrockets, there are several practical aspects to consider. We have a house to prepare for our departure, find a new school, a beloved dog to be taken care of, and luggage to pack. The magnitude of the task before us is daunting. However, the anticipation of the journey we are about to undertake balances it all. Fortunately, we have a few months to prepare for our official departure, and to plan and make all the necessary arrangements to undertake this project in peace. A whirlwind of activity was activated in the following weeks. I take care of organizing every detail. It allows me to escape the daily hassles and worries of life in Calgary. Following my husband's suggestion, our trip was to start in Quito, Ecuador to visit his family. However, the plans move in a different direction. The first part of our trip will now be dedicated to relaxing, making connections and exploring new cultures in Europe.

Turnaround from the start

At the end of May 2014, our adventure began. The feeling of detachment brings freedom to the heart. Space is being created for the discoveries that lie ahead. It is a year to learn and grow, to immerse ourselves in various countries, languages, and cultures. Our journey begins with a flight to the amazing city of Venice, Italy. To our delight, my mother joins us for a memorable cruise. For a month, we explore a myriad of destinations: Turkey, Greece, France, Italy, and Spain. After my mother returned to Quebec, we continued to explore Spain. Several cities are charming. However, it is Barcelona that captures our initial interest. After having done the complete tour, we choose to settle in Alicante, a city located in the southeast of Spain. It is a peaceful and prosperous environment. This is where we enroll our twins in school. The Lycée Français offers a consistent curriculum. This allows students to study in a similar way to how they teach around the world. The children have the privilege of practicing Spanish more extensively, in addition to the English and French they're use to in Calgary.

However, our idyllic life in Alicante takes an abrupt turn. On a quiet evening, I receive a telepathic message from my grandfather. The urgency of his words is striking:

— "Anick, you have to get out of here."

— "We just arrived!" I reply.

His answer is clear:

— "You have to go to Ecuador now, Anick! Listen to me: it is absolutely necessary to leave as soon as possible."

The seriousness of his message is somewhat alarming. As soon as my surprise wore off, I passed on the warning to my husband. He understands my intuition and the need to consider the opinion of my guides. With remarkable efficiency, he sets about planning our sudden departure. I inform the school of our unexpected and imminent move.

In the blink of an eye, everything is set in motion. The next morning, we set off for another unexpected leg of our journey. As the month of August draws to a close we arrive in Quito. This capital is located in the Andes, at an altitude of more than 2,850 meters (9,350 feet) above sea level. Making it the second highest capital city in the whole world. We rent a villa in the serene suburb of Cumbaya. The opulence of nature blows us away. This haven is a true paradise with abundant fruit trees and a remarkable number of flowers adorning our garden. Avocados, lemons, and tamarillos are just a few of the delicacies we pick for our morning juices. In addition, the children's school is not far away by car. What a perfect place to rest and integrate the unforeseen events of a trip of a lifetime!

Transformation

The climate of this country is a constant embrace of warmth and sunshine throughout the year. Temperatures usually hover between 20 and 28 degrees Celsius. The days are illuminated by a radiant sun. It is essential to protect yourself with hats or scarves. Mornings bring the refreshing, invigorating and pure breath of the mountains with daylight starting at 6 a.m. Night falls just after 6 p.m. At this time, the temperature slowly drops below fifteen degrees Celsius. In the middle of the night, wrapped in a cozy blanket, we contemplate the magical and euphoric atmosphere created by the moon surrounded by stars.

During the first two weeks, I treat myself to the luxury of la *dolce vita*. Life is beautiful and I feel immensely happy. The kids are back in school, and my husband has the opportunity to reconnect with his family, catching up on the moments they've missed over the years. We celebrate life with small glasses of wine at aperitif time, cherishing the simple pleasures that abound in our tranquil environment. Everything works wonderfully and our hearts are overflowing with gratitude for all that is beautiful and good in our new life. Unfortunately, a virus infiltrates and disrupts the well-established serenity.

The first to fall ill was my daughter, followed by my son and me. The symptoms are similar to a severe flu with chills, body aches and fever. My husband, miraculously, was not affected. It is very likely that this is due to the antibodies he had developed as a child, being native to the region. For my part, I am intensely ill: I spend most of my days in bed. One night, I had been in bed and asleep for some time, and I had the strange feeling that my husband had entered the room and turned on the chandelier. However, light changes in intensity and quality, dancing, and twirls through my closed eyelids. After a few moments, I cautiously open my eyes and notice that it's not the ceiling light at all. An eccentric spark continues to intensify. My eyes quickly adapt to the shine. I then perceive a bright navy-blue sphere. A feeling of déjà vu emerges. Rays of pure white energy surge towards me. I can make out a small sparkle mixing with a soothing sky-blue hue. I hold my breath, determined not to miss a moment. Three radiant silhouettes of a pale fluorescent blue are formed. Each is at least seven feet tall. They have large, almond-shaped black eyes. They analyze my behavior. I can make out their little curved mouths that look funnily like a flower of life. I clearly identify their energies: one masculine vibration and two feminine. Naturally, I synchronize my breathing with theirs. I hesitate between the option of them having chosen this moment precisely or that I orchestrated it myself. Despite my initial desire to run away from the situation, the disease had weakened me so much that I cannot do anything but stay in bed. Their magnetizing eyes keep me in a pleasant trance. I immediately lose all identification of who I am and where I stand in the vast expanse of space and time.

Still in my bed, a feeling of transformation runs through me. I feel like I'm receiving a complete update, a reprogramming of my DNA. Every cell in my body undergoes a noticeable change. A part of me awakens, becomes more aware, and connects to a higher purpose. I am acutely aware of what surrounds me. All my senses are heightened. The novelty that amazes me is the taste of the pure and fresh air of the room: purer than I have ever experienced, even in the high mountainous regions. Thanks to the air that fills my lungs, I notice a different sense of renewal. I feel like hundreds of tentacles are activating on my body, each connected to a separate organ, associated with its own rhythmic pulsation. I can see the detail of the eyes of the Beings of Light: they are made up of countless tiny eyes just like those of the fly. Inside each facet, I see several pieces of information belonging to different timelines. Everything is there at the same time: I see myself in the present, in the past and in the future. Inside the inside of each facet is another smaller facet. On it, the infinite movement of geometric spirals following the Fibonacci flower sequence[3]. This vision is painful to sustain and pushes me to scan my gaze elsewhere to rest my eyes. In addition, I feel my blood boiling in my veins. The heat radiates everywhere at the same time and the next moment, a strange cold runs through me from the top of my head to cool me down. The image that comes to me is a transfusion of heavenly blood. Despite all the desire to move, I came to a complete standstill, as if locked in a block of ice.

Along with everything that's going on in my body, the electric energy of the blue silhouettes gradually eases my anxiety. At the same time, I receive words of great kindness transmitted telepathically. In the

---

[3] Reference to the visual of flowers whose total number of petals is a number that is found in the mathematical sequence discovered by Fibonacci

space around me, the power of the vibration increases. From the moment the vibration merges with me, I am nothing but immeasurable love. This is nothing like what I felt as a human on Earth. I sense feminine energies that transmit a sense of calmness. The masculine energy provides me with a flow of oxygen, helping my breathing which has momentarily suspended due to my astonishment. This moment leaves me truly moved. There is no time or room for fear: it no longer exists. Only wonder and tranquility.

— "We're sorry we came to you like this. We have a message."

Even if this is not my first encounter with Beings of Light, the experience disorients me every time:

— "Your body needs to undergo a purification process. The increase in all kinds of pollution of the planet has led to the accumulation of toxic substances in your body. Your ability to connect effectively with us has diminished. Only children naturally disintegrate this toxicity thanks to their higher vibrations. You are one of us. Before coming to Earth, you accepted an essential mission. You are the bridge between the Beings of Earth and us, the Beings of Light of the galaxy. We need your role as an intermediary to spread our message to the new generation of children of the New Earth. It's your role to help them integrate and teach them their missions. With your ability to manifest at the right time, you will be able to activate people who are attracted to your light. They will be mostly children. Do not dare to offer your help out of pity: darkness is watching you. Follow your intuition. We will guide you and send you the people who need to meet you. A lot is going to happen on your planet, and you won't always understand. Rest assured: you're in the right place at the right time. Don't worry, you'll have more information on the next steps."

As soon as the speech ends, the Blue Beings slowly dissolve one after the other through the ceiling of the room. Back to my human senses, I wonder how my children, who sleep next to me, could have not noticed this extraordinary moment. The brightness is like a persistent sun, under which it is difficult to stay. Even my husband, who is relaxing in the next room, remains perfectly oblivious to this visit from another dimension. I have the distinct impression that the Beings of Light are deliberately ensuring that I am the only one to perceive their presence. They probably have something to do with the deep sleep of my children... Again, I can't say how long that moment lasted. One thing is certain, I intend at all costs to join my husband to share what I have just experienced. With a weakened body, fighting a virus and in the midst of integrating this energetic intervention, my strength is limited. In addition, I have to take the time to get out of my trance state before getting up. On the way to the living room, I glance nervously over my shoulder. This is probably a signal from my surprised ego since I didn't feel any danger from my visitors. Worried, my husband asks me:

⏤ "Are you okay?"

I sit next to him, wrapped in my llama patterned duvet, and answer:

— "I don't know what's happening to me. I just experienced something incredible... It goes beyond words. Bright lights filled the room and woke me up. They surrounded me, just like when I was pregnant. I felt the same energy..."

I describe it the best as I can. After my story, snuggled up against my partner, a flood of memories resurfaces. A great sadness overwhelms me. I now have access to a buried fragment of my past, to a family and a reality that have shaped my existence from time to time. The realization of having forgotten them plunges me into a melancholy. How could I forget such an intense life? It all comes back to me: at six, I was at school on a spaceship, deciphering energies and DNA, and facilitating the activation of their new selves. I understood my mission. I have lived among Beings whose souls were not of this world. As the memories come one after the other, my subconscious finally opening up to my conscious self, I remember the pain I felt every day when I returned to my earthly family. In my eyes, it was just a family to learn from. At that time, the only consolation in my earthly existence was the presence of my sisters, one of whom was sick. I felt a responsibility to protect her when her energy waned. I always warned my mother when her energy dropped. I had a deep connection with my sisters. Unexpectedly, between my thoughts, I overhear a conversation between otherworldly beings. They discuss the consequences of going back and forth between my class and the spaceship, my role towards my sisters, and my energy exhaustion when resisting my return to Earth. It is possibly for all these reasons that access to these memories was only when I really needed them.

I notice that my husband is slightly surprised, but not disturbed by the description of the situation. He knows the incredible parts of my life well. Growing up in an open-minded environment, his mother instilled in him the belief that there are more than just humans living on Earth. In Ecuador, some individuals have had the chance to encounter

Beings from elsewhere. Such encounters are not uncommon. My husband confides that his mother reminded him that some people were specially destined to live through some strange or odd moments, precisely in order to tell them. This statement brings me great relief. It confirms to me that he understands me. Without judging, he accepts me in the entirety of my being. The next day, despite my ever-present tiredness, we went to my mother-in-law's house. I tell her about my recent meeting. I expected her to be a little surprised. Nonchalant and amused, she adds:

— "I'm not surprised. My Beings of Light visit me every two to three months. They contact me to check on what's going on here and to share updates about my home planet, Ganymede. Let's not forget that here in the Ecuadorian mountains, we are the closest point on Earth to space."

Her revelation blows us away! We exchange a knowing look. This means that I am not alone in my ability to perceive and interact with these Beings. She turns to me and adds:

— "In any case, I have a premonition. You will witness the beauty that your children will bring to this planet."

I am amazed and delighted. She continues, addressing her son:

— "Remember the accident we had when you were just six years old? We were driving on a road late at night. Unexpectedly, I was completely blinded by two huge white lights that appeared in front of the car. It was such a big jolt. The vehicle rolled five to six times before coming to rest in the ditch. To the second, two men appeared. Seemingly out of nowhere, they saved us. They quickly took care of you and brought you back to our house. I remember very well my chills at the sight of your badly wounded and bloody head. We quickly discovered two holes on the top of your head. It was a nightmare situation. Strangely, you didn't feel any pain during the ordeal."

⊢ "Yes," my husband replies, "Your memories reflect mine. I remember being shaved and wrapped in a thick bandage. The images remained clear in my mind. I am convinced that these two men were Beings of Light from your planet. Thanks to them, we were rescued and saved from death."

Mesmerized by her words, we remained there: my husband also with a similar memory and I astonished by what has just been told. For his mother, convinced of the validity of these events, sharing this story seems as natural as discussing the weather. Over the next few days, I remain sick. My mind struggles with the plausibility of the discoveries that have recently come to light. Doubts try to intrude through the ego. Is this real?

As I recover, I realize that something has irrevocably changed in me. I can no longer tolerate certain foods or drinks that I loved just a few days ago. For example, the aroma of wine and coffee now elicits an aversive reaction. The consumption of meat is now incompatible with my being. My daughter, who has always been a vegetarian, is already on this path, which is the right one for her. I physically perceive things in a completely different way: the colors, the noises, the toxicity of food and especially the environment, the connections with animals and insects... These changes support the exact message conveyed by the Beings of Light. My life is increasingly embarking on a transformative trajectory. The intensity of my virus is in a way a process of purging impurities and toxic elements. I feel that a high frequency energy is gradually integrating into me. I decide to trust their wisdom and to continue by accepting all these changes in lifestyle. This is another period of discovery and adjustment.

The frequency of visits by the Beings of Light is increasing, sometimes in person and other times in the living landscapes of my dreams. Their words resonate in my mind:

⊢ "Anick, we are here with you!"

It's a sweet reminder. It is impossible to allege that their existence is a mere illusion. I am at the point where I clearly have to deal with this reality. I accept the connection I have with them. I want to understand the reasons for their support and find out the purpose of their presence. In accordance with their words, I perceive a definite improvement in my well-being. My children have also recovered from their microbe. Then, one night, a message from the Beings of Light reached me. My path took a new turn, which was to say that they urged me to leave for Quebec, Canada. The omen of a significant event awaits me there. Despite the unknown that raises a little stress, an unshakeable confidence in the advice received counterbalances the discomfort and allows a dose of serenity to emerge.

Chapter 10

A new way to help

The month of October brings us back to Quebec, Canada. The cold drizzle greets us as we get off the plane. The contrast with Quito's mild climate is striking. This temperature hovers around twelve degrees Celsius. My parents, delighted to see us, pick us up at the airport and drive us to our temporary home. We settle in a Swiss chalet style house. It is located next to my parents' residence. It's a place they've owned for several years. In no time, the decision is made to enroll the children in the elementary school that I attended as a child. If the entities of the cemetery resurface, I already intervened by enlightening my children on the subject. Questions persist about the advice that my Beings of Light have given me. Do they suggest that we stay longer or is it a brief stay, then, head elsewhere afterwards?

Returning to this place brings back an abundance of memories from my childhood. A mixture of emotions and apprehension is present in the face of what the future holds. My main goal is to take care of myself and rest. This is one of the messages received from the Beings more than a month ago. The important steps of settling down are well underway. Registrations went smoothly. The school gladly accepts them. My children join their classmates the next day. The first night in the cottage goes off without incident, although I feel the presence of entities that have inhabited the house for decades. I wake up full of energy and happy to prepare breakfast on this first day of school for the children. After dropping them off at school, my husband and I return to the car parked beside the nearby cemetery. The image of my childhood friend Hugo comes back to me. Nostalgic and lost in my thoughts, I don't notice the silhouettes approaching in the distance until I hear their voices. The shadows are gradually taking shape and I can distinctly hear their curious remarks about the changes that have taken place in me since our last meeting when I was a child. While I am conversing with my husband, mysterious characters who come near us implore me to introduce them to my children. I address them telepathically:

— "Hello, it's good to see you again! You have already seen my children Sofia and Enrique when we arrived. I ask you to respect their privacy and give them the space to adapt to their new environment, which is very different from what they have known. Please protect them as you did with me."

The unanimous commitment to look after my children is reassuring. Meanwhile, my husband notices my distraction and says:

— "You must have a lot of memories in this place."

— "Yes, for sure! I am convinced that our children will love this school."

The next day, while the children are at school and my husband is busy on the main floor, I decide to take some time to meditate in my bedroom on the second floor. The room offers the perfect ambience: when you open the curtains, the sweet scent of trees permeates the room. Fall is a comforting season for me because it is associated with wonderful times. The window offers a beautiful view of the river basking in the sunlight. I opt for a comfortable chair, with my feet anchored to the floor and my back straight. Taking three deep breaths, I exhale slowly, letting go of the agitation of my ideas in my mind. My body becomes lighter and in a few minutes my spirit rises. I feel free and invigorated. No longer being tied to my body, it's like I'm floating in the air. I find myself outside the room, beyond the confines of the house. I find myself floating in space. I admire the beauty that surrounds me. The view of Earth in orbit is breathtaking. Absolute tranquility reigns and a great serenity lives in me. It is at this moment that a message from the Beings of Light in Ecuador resonates in my mind:

— "You will help the children of the New Earth."

I am shaken by the immensity of the responsibility I have just been given. Questions are rushing around. Doubt revisits me. Who are these children? How would I recognize them? What can I do to help them? In a sudden movement, I find myself through the cosmos. Propelled by an invisible force, I fly. I revel in the feeling of weightlessness and explore the world at my leisure. My journey is abruptly interrupted by a powerful vibration that takes me downhill.

I materialized in a country, then in a city then finally in a house where a heartbreaking scene unfolds. A young girl around 3 years old is lying on a bed. Her parents are kneeling at her bedside, tears in their eyes. The extremely low energy I capture undoubtedly tells me that there is only a short time left before the child's life ends. For her last moments, the extended family stands around. As I observe the situation, I realize the untapped power they possess to heal the little girl. It involves forming a circle by holding hands. The channel created will allow the collective energy to transfer to the dying child. Unfortunately, her family is unaware of this ability. My role becomes clear: I have to absorb the little energy that remains and supplement it with my own to redirect it to the child. I melt into the middle of them, taking the form of a ball of radiant light. With my hands, I collect their vanishing energy and combine it with mine. I then direct this combination of vitalized vibrations towards the little girl. Through this process, I witness a miraculous transformation. Life resumes in the body without tone. The child's color returns and her eyes open. Her parents exchange astonished glances with each other. Hope is reborn in their hearts. Sobs give way to tears of happiness. My sense of accomplishment makes me realize that I had already begun my mission by working through dreams and meditations. It is time to make this mission conscious and to update it deliberately.

Chapter 11

Teaching on board the spaceship

Since the notion of time does not exist outside the earthly dimension, I continue to float in space. This moment spans hours, days, even months above the Earth. An exhilarating surge of energy flows through me. Amazed, I feel the infinite and soothing calm of vastness. So to speak, I have no desire to return, in spite of all the attractions of my earthly life. My children and husband are the only reasons that encourage me to come back. It is a pleasure for me to reveal to them the existence of this incredible state and to share the discoveries and knowledge related to it.

Every time I embark on an astral adventure, my energy is restored, ready to dive into another world. A particular sensation signals the departure for my dimensional journeys. Intense pain in my head, as if I was being hit brutally, indicates the beginning of my transition. My essence returns to its original form, which is a flickering light. The latter rises out of my body. As I circle the Earth, I harness the energy of the stars, the atmosphere, and the universe. In this way, I amplify it to connect with the Beings of Light. My goal is precise: to transmit pure light through my hands to children facing adversity. I wonder which countries need me today.

I feel so tiny in the middle of the vastness of space! A distant, slow, subtle, and serene noise disturbs the tranquility. The sound resonating in the cosmic silence is unknown to me. Becoming louder and louder and preceded by a low whistle, I wonder and scan the surroundings in search of its source. My curious gaze swivels in all directions. All of my senses are on the alert. To begin with, I see one, then another and soon a third spaceship. Each one slightly different, but strangely similar. Suddenly, a colossal object appears in my field of vision, silently approaching at a steady pace. It stops in front of me. It is a massive, yet elegant, oval-shaped vessel with a slightly flattened top crowned with a dome. Its presence hypnotizes me to such an extent that I no longer pay attention to the first vessels that appeared and are now positioned behind this one. The air smells of metal and the sound continues to buzz in my eardrums. The door of the great vessel lowers. From the intense white light that bursts forth, the shape of three silhouettes illuminated in vibrant blue emerges. These silhouettes are the same ones I encountered in Ecuador. Curiosity rises, nervousness runs away and doubt squirms in the back of my mind. I tell myself to stay calm and I keep telling myself that I'm only meditating, but sometimes reality is stronger than consciousness. No matter how much I rationalize, my restlessness persists. Aware of the need to keep my cool, I try to temper my anxiety. I feel the presence of two feminine energies and one masculine. Their peaceful auras reassure me. However, some apprehension remains. I fear that my obvious sense of being overwhelmed will keep them away and I desperately want to maintain their presence.

While I still stand in front of these Beings at the entrance of the ship, I repeat inwardly to welcome them with serenity and love. Everything will be fine. My heart wants to burst with happiness: I hold back a desire to shout the joy within me. How did they travel from Ecuador to Quebec? I thus become aware of what I had already understood in my childhood: from their point of view, a few minutes or seconds have passed since our last meeting. The concepts of distance and time as we know, do not exist for them.

As I turn my attention back to the present moment, my excitement grows despite my efforts to hide it. They signal me to come closer. I walk towards them and through the open door of their ship. A serenity runs through my being and my heart: the memory of our previous warm encounter calms me. The interior of the ship exudes an aura of immaculate cleanliness. Everything is white, translucent as if this ship had just been built for my arrival. The noticeable smell is a mixture of fresh scent and metal. The place seems to have never known an inhabitant. Everything materializes simultaneously in front of me with each of my steps. My head wonders how I can materialize everything I see if I haven't visited this place before. My eyes widen as I see a wide corridor stretching out in front of me. Everywhere I look, the majestic aspect of this place impresses me.

Among the Beings of Light, there are other entities of unknown appearance. I have a hard time defining their shapes: they are different from humans. Out of respect, I nod to them as a greeting. Meanwhile, my self-talk continues. I am amazed that I can stay in a wonderful place for so long. My thoughts connect with theirs, allowing for direct communication. Their comments among themselves reflect their incomprehension and questioning of my astonished reactions. The Beings wonder about the fact that I am not familiar with the surroundings, as if they expect me to know this place.

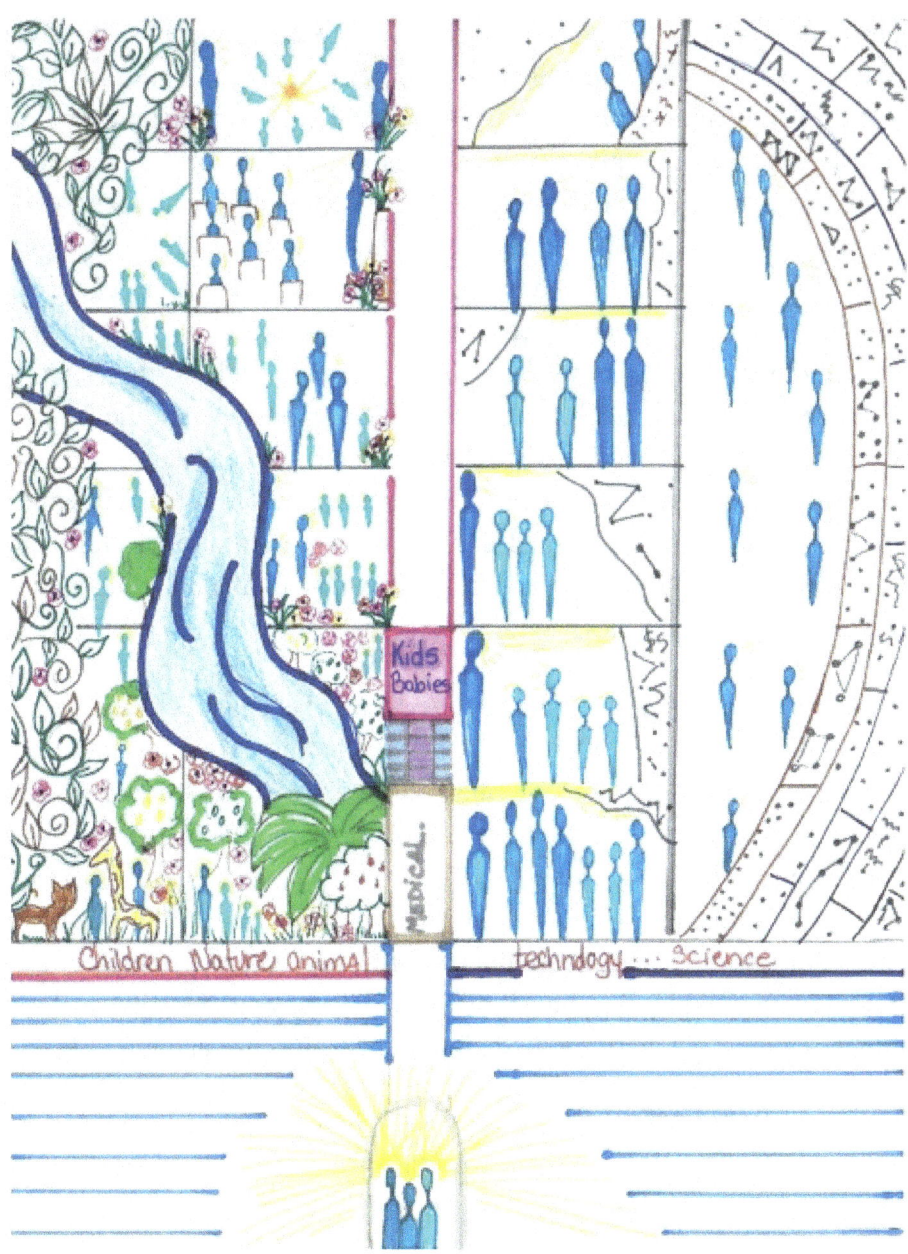

Children Nature animal

Kids Babies

MEDICAL

technology ... Science

I turn my gaze to the right and a multitude of large screens rise. Computers and various electronic devices fill the space. Further on, I notice a set of buttons and control panels accessible only to authorized personnel. As I try to make sense of my presence in this spectacular place, I wonder if it's the technology department or the ship's control center. It's teeming with individuals. The collective animation reminds me of an anthill. I turn my attention to the left. The view of the technology department dissolves and is replaced by an environment focused on nature and vegetation. My senses absorb the vibrations and smells known in the City of Light that I find in various countries visited. The energy of trees, animals and the earth accompanied by the smell of its humidity join my vibration. The air is soft and pure: freshness with every breath. A light scent of lilacs and roses enhances the passage of the breeze. Gigantic trees surround me. I approach a water source. The sound of the trickling is delicate to my ears. In the distance, I hear voices commenting on my presence among them. These curious creatures are watching me. The more I continue my journey in the department, the more the feeling of unity with nature grows.

I am once again capturing the telepathic exchanges of the Beings of Light. They wonder why I react this way today. They sense my inner turmoil. I want to keep some semblance of control. A mixture of sadness and happiness appears; I see that I am the one who has forgotten. I find myself exactly where I have been going in my meditations for years. With a bit of sadness, I can't believe they left me on Earth for so long. Why did it take so long to reconnect with me? An immense feeling of abandonment rises in my thoughts. Why this long wait? I resolve to focus more on the gratitude of finally being in their presence again.

The return of my memory is doing its work. I recognize the destination: I am guided to the children's section. I question their insistence on going through the "medical" section when there is another direct route to the youth zone. Maybe they're thinking about familiarizing me with the layout of the departments or rehashing the events I experienced in class on the ship, when I was six years old. I pass in front of the closed medical department. Its sterile wards are devoid of energy. I follow my guides in silence. We arrive at a lifting platform. It is an open glass structure with a full view from top to bottom. When I'm on board, I instantly transport up. The ground floor is now tiny under my feet: twenty floors have been climbed. Once the platform is stopped, we take a corridor. I recognize very well what surrounds me: the children's section. The many classrooms extend on either side. The Blue Beings stop in front of me. They open the door and signal me in. They close it and stay outside the room. The room is filled with young Blue Beings children. Their presence is not unknown to me. I wonder about my role here. Naturally, I walk to the front of the class. I sit on the edge of the desk, taking on a rather familiar role. With a puzzled look, I observe the Blue children who fix their attention on me. They, too, wonder why I seem distant and hesitant.

— "What's going on, madam? Just yesterday, you were perfectly fine! Why do you seem surprised to see us?"

My human brain persists in questioning:

— "What? Was I here yesterday?"

I remember that the notion of time has no influence here and that the concept of yesterday is relative... At the same time, I think about what I am supposed to share or teach these Blue Beings. I'm sure they already know everything. My thoughts are abruptly interrupted. A blinding white screen materializes in my mind, rendering my usual thought processes useless. An intense blue light laser radiates from each child's third eye and converges on mine. The dozen beams merge into a wave so powerful that I can barely stand it. My whole body is shaking. Something enters me with force. The feeling is more than unpleasant, I would even say uncomfortable.

My head shakes subtlety from side to side. My closed eyes flicker tremendously. A restlessness is felt in the chakra of my head, and I feel goosebumps running through as if it were tentacles. Electric shocks rush through both my arms. I hold my breath in a desperate attempt to absorb the information being conveyed. All around me, I hear noises, sounds, and several strange languages that remind me of something. There are also many images intermingled: numbers, symbols, and colors. A flood of data pulses towards my third eye at an uncanny speed. I can't take it anymore. The Blue Beings must have sensed my distress. All the lasers go out simultaneously and this shattering experience ends quickly. I breathe in loudly, a bit like a swimmer out of breath when rising to the surface of the water. Tears stream down my face. I am perfectly aware that there are Beings in the room. I silently force myself to regain my composure and stifle my sobs. I have the impression that their gaze is probing me. I think it probably only lasted about a minute or two.

Despite my efforts to hide the powerful emotions that shook me, tears roll down my cheeks. I look up cautiously, observing the three Beings of Light waiting by the classroom door. Their telepathic message reaches me:

⊢ "Anick, it's an exchange you've been doing since you were a child. The difference is that today is the first day that you are aware of this event. You have to share it with the humans on Earth."

I get up from the desk on which I am still leaning on. I nod my head in gratitude to the children before leaving the room. In the hallway, three more Blue Beings materialize and join their counterparts on my right side. Thus, I find myself at the center of a protective circle. Kind words end up in my ears.

⊢ "Anick, don't worry! We understand how humans feel here. They often seem lost, as if they are here for the first time. Humans tend to forget and their memories fade. You'll see, you'll remember what you experienced here. Relax. Don't dwell on anything. We are delighted and your presence is precious among us."

Unexpectedly, an energetic force takes hold of my body. It's as though there is a time limit, and the allotted time has been exceeded. With a swift movement, I am catapulted to Earth, re-entering my body in an instant. I open my eyes and realize that I am sitting in the armchair in my bedroom. The grandeur of the journey I have just made is striking and my eyes overflow with emotion. Baffled, I keep repeating to myself: "What am I doing here? What happened to me? I feel like I've spent hours in the spaceship. Yet, as I check the clock, I realize that no more than twenty minutes have passed since I began my meditation. The sudden urge to go to the bathroom brings me back completely "with both feet on the ground". The contrast is striking between the terrestrial dimension and that of the spaceship in which there is an absence of bodily needs. Having regained my senses, I return to myself, this time superimposing a little more easily all my roles on earth: that of a mother, fulfilled wife and mysterious woman linking the Earth and the cosmos.

As a result of this meditation, a veil of a facet of my existence is definitively lifted. Situations forgotten or voluntarily erased by my guides resurface. I remember the sensational encounters I have had since childhood. I remember my astonishment at the age of six when I met Beings so different from me. I also remember the first time I saw my children in the energy dimension. I realize that my soul has always known them, even if my conscious memory has been erased. This is both eccentric and joyful. From now on, I remember to go even further forward.

Chapter 12

The Blue Being that I am!

My meditative journeys are emotionally charged. Each time I return, I seek comfort and understanding by confiding in my husband. He has always been my confidant, offering me unwavering support. Although he finds my experiences intriguing, I am certain that he genuinely believes in me.

In the days that follow, the redundancy of the questions that populate my thoughts is still as active as ever. The desire to live again within the spaceship and bring healing to the children obsesses me. "I need to meditate again!" I thought to myself. Back in the same room upstairs, I settle into the meditation routine. Sitting on the narrow couch that belonged to my grandmother, I close my eyes, I go down inside me and I settle there. I see myself being thrown out of my physical body. I am going through energy planes in stages. Soaring around the planet, I send a white light of healing to children in need. Once I reach the top of the Earth, I wait excitedly for the sound of the approaching ship to be heard. I love this noise which brings back a feeling of welcome. As expected, the spaceship arrives, finally! The door opens and I go inside. This time, there was no overwhelming emotion. Only serenity... I begin to follow my guides.

Not far from the entrance is the technological section of the ship. Unforeseen, I am surprised by what I perceive: my son, in an adult version, who naturally performs telekinesis from one object to another or directly in his hand. In addition, everyone around him in this work section does too! Stunned, I continue to follow the Beings. We reach the section dedicated to vegetation and animals. I see my daughter in her adult version! She transmits energy to many animals. It is a bit unsettling to meet your own children in a version not known in this realm!

Back in the classroom with the young Blue Beings, I take my place in the front desk with confidence. The children start to transmit their data lasers again. This session seems even more intense than the last few times. I want to know what has changed because everything is moving at an accelerated pace. The volume of information I accumulate is amazing. A wide range of topics are listed: changes in DNA, adaptation to the new vibrational frequencies transitioning between dimensions (from the third to the fifth) and the urgent need to take care of our planet (for water and our food supply). It's huge, somewhat overwhelming flow of knowledge. I try to record as much as possible, but it's impossible to capture everything.

My body and mind are particularly tired from this moment in class. Once the transmission is over, I express my gratitude to the children. I head outside the classroom where six Beings of Light are waiting for me. This time, my heart is filled with bliss. I have the irresistible urge to give them a hug, despite the time that is passing quickly. I know that my presence here is for a limited time. Taking a step forward, I stretch out my arms to hug one of the Beings of Light: I see my hand go through it without touching anything. All the Beings look at me with an uncertain expression. In another attempt, I offer a handshake, raising my arm to one of theirs. A sphere of energy materializes between our palms. When I see its eyes, I am completely magnetized. In this penetrating gaze, I contemplate the entire universe, life, death, pain, ecstasy, and the immensity of the infinite. Its eyes display the colors of the globe. Inside them, I see my future self, my present self and my past self in the form of miniature images.

In the middle of this magical moment, I glance at my hand close to the Being. I notice that it is tinged with vibrant blue that looks funnily like itself. Immediately, I look at my body and realize that I am entirely blue.

⊢ "Is it possible? Am I a Blue Being?"

⊢ "Yes, Anick, you have always been one of us. That's why you feel at home."

In this exchange, my third eye establishes a connection with it. I realize that this is how we say goodbye in this dimension. The intensity of the knowledge transmitted exhausts me. I am both euphoric and melancholic. Being with the Blue Beings on their ship brings me pure joy. Having to leave them brings me back to this feeling of loss of the functioning of this dimension. Flooded with gratitude, I thank them for accompanying me and teaching me. I hear them reply:

⊢ "Thank you! Goodbye! You can come back whenever you want, Anick. It's your home."

For them, it is not a one-time encounter, but rather a daily communion with our earthly territory. They are interconnected with us, residing in a parallel dimension beyond our perception, unless we lift the veil that separates our worlds.

At this point, they conceive that I am living a "human" moment, far removed from the nature of a "Blue Being". So, as a matter of course, I need a reminder of the teachings I have forgotten. They are well aware of our choice to incarnate on Earth and the need to erase our memory. This is the case for living our human experiences fully and freely. The moment the ego tries to grasp these concepts, confusion ensues. Returning to Earth after my visits to the ship usually leaves me with a powerful sense of abandonment. It's an emotional rollercoaster that I'm finding harder and harder to bear.

I realize that many others certainly have a similar experience, but do not remember it. I consider myself lucky to have access to it. I'm thrilled to be reminded again that I'm part of their family.

Fascination

Reconnecting with this family brings me the desire to keep it all omnipresent. Their world is a persistent interest in my daily life. It is impossible to deny this. My earthly responsibilities and obligations do not allow me enough time to meditate. I do this briefly here and there when I can take the time.

The travel opportunities with my husband are nice escapes. It's great for rekindling our romance from before we had children. It's also a joy for the children because they can spend time with their grandparents. This respite for the well-being of our family offers us a harmonious balance. During the school holidays we go on adventures by taking trips and cruises in the Caribbean. These precious moments allow us to nurture and strengthen the bonds between us.

Nevertheless, the spirits and the deceased continue to reach out to me. They detect my presence wherever I am. Not having the same social filters as us, they come to me, no matter the moment. I feel their emotions and their sadness, which forces me to help them in order to feel better in turn. In every place we visit, I receive information and messages to convey in addition to the teachings of my guides that I integrate. These adaptations are sometimes demanding. Sometimes I lose interest in daily activities and find comfort only in my meditation. This morning ritual has become a lifeline to a world where I feel the desire to find myself in.

As the winter sets in with its cold embrace, it becomes less and less pleasant to venture outside. Usually, the idea of enjoying a hot drink in a café with my spouse in Old Quebec City is alluring. Instead, I find myself hoping to meditate. This activity has become a form of personal therapy. Up there, I feel an indescribable tranquility. Each time, the transition to the Earth plane leaves me thinking: "What am I doing here?" From this point of view, I wonder about the reasons for my choice to experience the world here on earth. I watch my husband and children go about their business and sometimes I am reluctant to return to Earth. A whimsical thought crosses my mind: I wish I could take them on the spaceship. We could live together and never have to come back. It's an unachievable extravagance, but the desire is undeniable. Almost every day, I immerse myself in meditation. It's a routine that has become sacred. I spend at least 20 minutes meditating before embarking in other activities. This leaves me slightly lethargic afterwards. My husband suggests that I change my routine or go out of the house to enrich my meditations. While I understand his point of view, I am not convinced. My meditations are my top priority. Despite his continued support, this frustrates him at times. My spouse encourages me to do something else to get out of the intense cycle of introspection that I have created. He kindly repeats to me that balance is necessary in all aspects of life. So I decide to follow the advice of my precious ally.

Reinstatement

My guides have their own way of rewarding me. They offer surprises like low-cost last-minute trips to interesting destinations such as Paris, London, and Arizona. Through these favors, they guide me and tell me where I have to go next. I recognize that I am fortunate to have these opportunities. On several occasions, fascinating anecdotes are intertwined. It's an original way to teach me valuable lessons and remind me of the importance of my mission on Earth.

One trip, which stands out in particular, takes place in Paris in the company of my husband. At Charles de Gaulle airport, we hurry to the boarding gate for our flight that was about to board bound for London. Caught in the whirlwind of last-minute boarding preparations, a detail catches my eye: a girl about eight years old sits alone on a bench appearing lost. A whisper in my ear prompts me to approach her. I ask her softly:

— "Are you okay? Are you lost? Are your parents with you?"

Frozen by fear, the young girl manages to answer in French:

— "I lost my mother. I thought I was following my stepdad, but he was a different gentleman." Her eyes fill with tears and panic sets in.

Taking a soothing tone, I reassure her:

— "Don't worry. We will find her again. Do you believe in guides, angels, or fairies? Call them, imagine them around you, they will come to help you. Think of your mom. Focus, and you'll attract her."

The terminal, vast and full of people, complicates things. We are on the second floor and her mother can be anywhere in this dense crowd. Seeing a security guard in the distance, we approach him, desperately looking for help. To my surprise, he informs me that he cannot make an announcement. Time is running out; the departure of our plane is imminent. Frustration and urgency take hold of me. So, I decide to contact my guides urging them to delay our flight to England. I am resolute. They are required to help me, otherwise I don't fly. Ten minutes later, I notice the little girl looking at a woman in the distance. I ask her if it's her mother. Uncertain but hopeful, we approach the woman. I call her:

— "Madam! Madam!"

She turns around and their eyes meet. It's her mother... The reunion is moving! Now that the family is reunited, I am pleased. I offer them my blessings:

— "Stay together now. Take care of each other. You will have a wonderful life, little one. Good luck!"

Happy to have played a role in their reunion, I quickly join my husband who is waiting for me a little bit in the background with our luggage. The flight attendants call us on the microphone. The plane is still there! As I board the plane, I hear in my mind:

— "You see, Anick, we need you on Earth!"

My guides demonstrate my reason for being here.

Chapter 13

My Beings from the Stars

Since our reunion in Ecuador, I have realized that my encounters with these Blue Beings are not mere serendipitous events. Each encounter is a key to unlocking another dimension of my life going back to the moment of my birth. In fact, they have always been there, like a whispered presence from the depths of my subconscious, guiding me through the labyrinth of life.

In the calm of the night, a recurring dream remains mysterious. This dream contains fragments of the beginning of my life as a human baby. I see myself in a state nursery[4], swaddled in a beige blanket like all the others around me. The cradles are made of glass. The name of each baby and its date of birth are directly engraved on the head of the cot. Among the female humans present, I also notice there are Blue Beings. Serene, they watch over us with a gaze filled with love and gentleness. My heart beats with curiosity and confusion. Why am I here? Where are my parents? These questions remain unanswered. I see a woman cradling a newborn baby. Looking at her, I can feel all the tenderness that envelops this precious young life. At the foot of my cradle, a supernatural glow captures my attention. The silhouette of a Blue Being with a vibrant presence attracts me. This link is rather familiar to me. We have crossed paths before. Through the gaze of her luminous eyes, a wave of emotion shakes me: a sense of belonging and connection as if I had finally come home. Like the flicker of a flame that is lit, I see a code of celestial energy transferring from the Being to my infantile Self. This silent custodian has been by my side since the first beat of my heart on the earthly plane. A lingering question resumes: why don't I see my human parents? Wouldn't I deserve their love? The uncertainty and pain of abandonment come back to pierce me with a vengeance. The happiness of being surrounded

---

[4] A place where children who had been abandoned, whose parents could not take care of them and usually run by nuns until 1978

by people and Beings is overshadowed by the sadness and the emptiness left by my parents. I am visited by opposing emotions that intertwine in a delicate dance, each in turn leading the pace.

I wake up with the morning light filtering through the curtains. The fragments of emotions bring back the same questions: why was I in this place? Why have I been entrusted to strangers, surrounded by infants in cribs, some of whom are wrapped in the same soothing glow as I am?

One night, in a quiet moment in the company of my grandfather's spirit, the pieces of the puzzle begin to fall into place. He provides me with the missing elements to give meaning to this vision. My grandfather speaks in a low voice. His voice tinged with sadness that is similar to mine. My parents were unprepared to take on all the responsibilities of my unexpected arrival. They were barely eighteen years old. The fear of social rejection, shame and worry of judgment by others weighed heavily on them. With these considerations, they decided to leave me in the state nursery for a few weeks after I was born. Of course, it will forever change the course of my life. But I have no resentment towards them. I understand the weight of the burden at a time when such circumstances were taboo. Society's critique was harsh and unforgiving towards those who deviated from its expectations. In their own way, they did what they thought was best for me. On one hand, a cosmic conception escapes my human comprehension. On the other hand, I understand that this is part of the plan I accepted before incarnating to discover who I am.

In the crib, while in the soft glow of the Beings of Light, I am infused with comfort. I am bordered by a sense of belonging that transcends earthly kinship ties. Their love, though different from that of a human parent, is no less real or deep. It sustained and fulfilled me during those first days without contact and affection of my human family. It is in this sacred moment that a spark of ancient wisdom ignites in me. I understand... These Beings are not mere visitors crossing the tapestry of my life in a punctual way; they are an integral part of my very essence.

Their light is intertwined with mine. An immense joy floods my heart. I finally understand why they feel like old friends and why their presence is as natural to me as my heartbeat.

As I grew, my connection with them developed subconsciously through my dreams, meditations, and night flights. Always guided with wisdom, it was with them that I went beyond the limits of this earthly realm where love flowed freely. In my younger years, it was easier for me to find happiness in their world. Our earthly dimension is marked by competition and the constant pursuit of something *"more"*.

At the dawn of a new chapter in my life, I take with me the knowledge of who I am and where I come from. This fits perfectly with the reasons why I am here. The fascinating thing is that they are always present with us. Their invisible presence is palpable to me. I am a child of the cosmos, chosen for a purpose that extends far beyond the limits of the child of the Earth that I also embody. I'm not the only one: I'm convinced that other people are like me. The inability to perceive Blue Beings can be the result of individual mandates or life missions. If building an intense relationship with them does not match the "tools" needed for our mission on Earth, it will not be part of our experience. Instead, other talents or skills will develop to serve the individual's unique path.

Now, I assume my true identity. For sure, I know that there is no going back. Dialogue and exchange of knowledge that flows freely between us has become second nature to me. I am amazed at their eagerness and overflowing joy at every contact we make. I can't explain to myself what I can bring to them as a human who recognizes herself as being from the stars!

My encounter with a Grey Being

As my guides mentioned, not all encounters with otherworldly Beings are warm. For some people, contacts can take a darker turn or leave them perplexed. On Earth, this negative perception is directly linked to the many myths. Over the centuries, these fables have structured and induced people to consider them as malicious entities.

I clearly remember a brief exchange with a Grey Being that occurred between waking and sleeping. This happened after the birth of my children:

— "I'm here to tell you that you're a copy of us. We are "you" in another dimension who have struggled to survive. It is of utmost importance to take care of yourself, cherish your planet, and communicate with all living and non-living beings."

Blue Beings and Grey Beings, in fact all Beings, are reflections of ourselves. They are an advanced or non-advanced version of our own existence, depending on the choices made in the different time slots that vary from one dimension to another. In reality, we attract what we vibrate and we attract situations to learn. Some have a low vibration. Although, short-lived, the encounter with the Grey Being left an indelible mark on my mind. Even today, its words resonate with me and awaken an awareness, transforming my relationship with my environment. Its message, simple but serious, speaks of our interdependence – not only with each other as living beings on the planet – but with the entire cosmos. There is no separation. We are all intimately connected to it in the history of its existence beyond the limits of our human imagination.

Chapter 14

Kid Avatars

The New Earth resonates with unconditional love and exceptional beauty. There are a very large number of Avatar children living there. Those I call Avatars have special abilities. Humanity defines them only as people with disabilities: physical and intellectual disabilities, mental health impairments, neurodivergence, language disorders, learning disabilities, visually impaired etc. Here, in the reality of the third dimension, the functioning of society is focused on competition, performance, doing, having, and appearing.

Avatars are destined to live in higher dimensions because the energy of our world is too dense for them. They are unable to demonstrate their true potential or gifts. Courageously, during the day, they make a real effort to integrate into our community. These young people exhaust themselves trying to conform to expectations and norms that do not correspond to their true essence. This can lead to other problems: devaluation, low self-esteem, demotivation, feeling of being part of nowhere, and so on. No matter what kind of difficulties they are struggling with, their role is important and much bigger than you can imagine. Let me explain how.

From my point of view, Avatar children possess a sensibility that few people know or understand. This allows them to perceive the world in a totally different way than the majority of the people around them. With heightened extrasensory perception, these small, full-fledged individuals see beyond Earth's density into other dimensions. They carry within them an energy that facilitates their existence in these other dimensions. Their presence on Earth has a specific purpose: to build this New World characterized by peace, light, unconditional love, and abundance, where scarcity has no place. They hold the key to the evolution towards this era that is upon us.

Unfortunately, the lack of understanding in most communities, the lack of resources and support for families and schools means that Avatar children are sometimes medicated. Stimulants impair or suppress their exceptional abilities. I'm not here to judge the choice of whether or not to use medication. It has its usefulness, although it's mostly convenient for the parents. Every child's development is different and sometimes there are no other choices available. However, it is important to know the consequences.

It is very likely that, in the New Earth, the use of that medication is no longer necessary. Their vibrations will be in accordance with the New World. Their roles will be reversed. They will become "the doctors". They will be the energy professionals of the transition to help us adapt to this dimension. Their contribution is essential in the transformation of our world, in the emergence of this new era. Moreover, their work has already begun. These wonderful Avatar beings are an integral part of the cosmic energy and accompany us on this journey, since we all originate from the stars.

Their mission: Our warriors on Gaia

The greatest mission of the Avatar children is to be protective warriors here on earth. This is reflected in their ability to absorb and transmute negative energies. The goal is to harmonize emotions and decrease the anxiety of people across humanity. Our warriors all possess this skill. Then, they improve the frequency of our planet. To do this, the Avatar children meet at night. While they sleep, their souls come together. No matter where they come from, they come together to serve common goals: to heal the planet, to harmonize the elements of all the systems that make it up (including us!), to coordinate earths grid to set it in place, and to expand the consciousness of those who inhabit it.

Each warrior emits their distinct melody. The energies synchronize to create a powerful symphony. It serves to regulate us by increasing the frequency of our environment. Coded messages can be found in this concert which is specially designed for us. Grouped by specific tasks, these little missionaries will transmit a beneficial energy that supports all the visible and invisible elements of the Earth: trees, flowers, insects, animals, Earthlings, bodies of water, fire, earth, air, fairies, gnomes, etc. Others use this energy to support the elderly. People who are about to leave their bodies receive reassuring energy. Some are assigned to victims of violence to comfort them. Soldiers in combat also receive this energy in order to try to do things differently. In short, warriors are walking around to raise the frequencies. Sometimes it doesn't work 100%. Why, you ask?

It must be remembered that, like you and me, the Avatar children and the victims have signed a contract to experiment. Free will was determined by the soul before coming here. The grand plan was made before incarnating through our parents and the lineages associated with them. All lives happen at the same time. Now, the adjustments are made gradually according to our reactions and choices to what is presented to us.

Through the tireless work and collective effort of these protectors, we are supported to lift the veil more easily from our eyes and consciousness and perceive the extraordinary City of Light. Specifically, our warriors on Gaia are representatives of the Cities of Light unknown to most humans. One of their related tasks is to welcome the children who arrive in the City of Light. Indeed, the Avatars are in the foreground. Their touch allows the healing of the rescued victims who arrive by the rescue ships.

In the Cities of Light, there are no judgments, no rigid rules, and no prescribed molds to fit into. It's a place where everyone can just be themselves. Children Avatars, Crystals, Indigo, etc., all come from a City which is their true home before being born in human form. It is a place of exquisite freedom. As they prepare for "another life," these souls are fully aware that their energy does not quite align with the vibrational density of life on Earth. Their arrival in the earthly land consists of accomplishing the objectives already enumerated, but also of solving karmas and making spiritual teachings.

Compared to the so-called "normal" children embodied in the matrix who use two strands of DNA, children from the City of Light often have twelve strands activated. Hence their different perception, their hypersensitivity, and their gifts. It is also the origin of their difficulties in functioning in our reality.

I know a few Cities of Light, but I am aware that there are many others around the world. These exceptional children who live there are waiting for the perfect moment to join the people who believe in their mission. Whether it's parents, a grandparent, an uncle, an educator, or a friend. Avatars reach people who, consciously or not, have grasped their essence. Those with whom the connection is natural and self-evident.

Love, harmony, interconnection with all living things are the foundations of the Cities of Light. It is a world where people coexist peacefully, caring for mutual well-being and engaging in collective healing. This is exactly what the Avatars, Gaia's warriors, are guiding us towards. Now that we know who they are and why they are among us, we should be deeply grateful to them.

Chapter 15

The stars and their language

YouTube: Light Language Ancestry

In June 2015, our sabbatical year comes to an end. My husband offers me one last adventure in Hawaii before returning to the rigors of everyday life. The energy of this place is nothing short of exceptional. In addition, without logically knowing the reasons, a strong bond seems to have been forged between the inhabitants of the islands and our family. Since the birth of our children, we have felt the need to be in this place to reconnect with this land and the people. In light of this, I realize that the lineage of these people resonates particularly with my children.

One night in Kauai, my sleep is punctuated by visits from various spirits. Among them, there are Beings who are unlike any I have ever met before. A well-established and indisputable hierarchy emerges through their presence. They establish contact with me in a language that I have already heard. Not understanding the words irritates me. It's not by getting angry that I'll be able to get the message. So, I decide to calm my thoughts to be more available. In the silence of my consciousness, the vibrations of the message are energetically transmitted to the cells of my being. Instantly, I grasp everything without interpreting or reasoning. It's a new and different way of working. This way of processing information is now accessible at all times. Before leaving, I get the following message:

― "From now on, this interplanetary language is encoded in you. Human words are incredibly limited that now we are required to speak in our language to help humanity. All terrestrial beings and living organism of any kind (humans, animals, plants, or any other species) can assimilate this language. It is the veil covering the planet that prevents Earthlings from accessing this knowledge."

The meaning of this message remains undefined for a very long time for me. Left in suspense without any other information, worry begins to wonder in my mind.

The next morning, as the tropical sun shines in all its glory, my husband takes our kids to the beach. I find a desired solitude to revel in the calm that surrounds me. I sit in the mezzanine with the French windows wide open sipping a jasmine-scented tea. Everything is enchanting and perfect: the sound of the ocean waves, their blue-green hue, the melody of the birds and the gentle sea breeze. This atmosphere of peace and tranquility is the perfect backdrop for my meditation. I look at the horizon, ready to embark on an inner journey that will, I hope, turn out to be fantastic.

It is in this sublime Hawaiian atmosphere that unknown sounds, utterances that resonate like a babble of unrecognizable words bursting out. These intriguing and powerful tones come from myself. I discover a completely new vocal expression with which I make no effort and which no thought precedes. I abandon myself to the phenomenon, even if the meaning of what I produce escapes me. That's not all. Something inexplicable happens: my hand starts to move without me consciously commanding it. Apparently, the hand performs gestures of its own free will. My fingers move as if I were at the keyboard of an invisible computer. I don't understand what's going on. I become more and more aware of my hand. It is surprising that it does not cause me any discomfort, no pain or fatigue. The notion of time has once again vanished. I open my eyes to the world around me: a little more than twenty minutes have passed. I can't stop the rise of anxiety. Crazy ideas are rattling. I wonder if this is not a symptom of an illness. What if this is an early stage of Parkinson's disease? In order to refocus my thoughts and calm down, I decide to go outside to breathe the fresh air directly on the edge of the ocean. As I walked to the beach where my husband and children were, the memory of the message I couldn't make sense of resurfaced:

— "This language is now integrated and activated in you."

Suddenly, an idea to explain the situation arises. Is this strange language the one that the Beings have presented to me? With a feeling of apprehension, I join my husband.

— "I'm not entirely sure what's going on," I confessed. "During my meditation, I began to make incoherent sounds and speak with unfamiliar words. What's even more worrying is that my hand was moving on its own. It seems as if the vibrations of my vocal tones synchronize with the movements of my hand. The two seem to act together. Strange, I admit, but that's what I just experienced."

As I chat with my husband, our six-year-old daughter turns to me with her eyes shining with wisdom beyond her years. With an optimistic look, she said to me:

— "Mama, it's energy in your hands. Rub your hands together and place them on me. You will feel the information that you are now ready to pass on."

I am stunned by the clearly articulated explanations of such a young child who understands the situation. It seems as if she has been prepared all her life for this intense moment of mine. I have already seen time and time again that my children have amazing abilities and knowledge. It still throws me off balance every time it happens. In response to her suggestion, I approach her and close my eyes. Gently placing my hands over her body, I feel an immediate change. I am transported out of the physical realm to join a powerful energy. I recognize a familiar poignant pain in my head, a sign of my departure for other dimensions. Panic starts to set in: this is absolutely not the time to do this in the middle of the beach in front of my children! Fortunately, things are looking different. I merge with my higher Self by surrendering to this new power. I look at my daughter's body through the eyes of my higher Being and a staggering picture emerges in front of me. Inside it, I see the whole universe. Against an infinite backdrop of stars and electric currents, millions of galaxies appear. It's breathtakingly beautiful. There are simply no words to describe what I see.

At the same time, the unknown language is activated inside my being. My hands start moving again on their own, guided by the energy that runs through me. My daughter's different vibrations intertwine in my palms. I let my hands slide gently over her body while feeling the back and forth of the undulations. My movements reflect these fluctuations. Whenever there is resistance, my hand adjusts so that a smooth connection is made. I continue to make a series of strange and incomprehensible sounds. I feel like I'm speaking in several languages simultaneously. The initial panic has given way to wonder. Despite my lack of control over the situation, I feel an unwavering sense of confidence, as I feel guided by my Higher Self. It's fascinating. After placing my hand at the height of her navel, the sounds I make are very similar to the frequencies of a poorly tuned radio. A force is deployed from the navel. It begins to rotate as it widens, forming a funnel. In this vortex, I see all my ancestors. The next moment, they surround us. Impressed and very enthusiastic to see them again, they tell me the following:

— "The belly button is an extremely powerful energetic door. All manifestation passes through the navel and not through the brain. It's a place to be protected. Your "genius" in you resides there. People attracted to who you are can siphon off some of your strength that makes up this vortex. Be sure to cover it up around people who make you uncomfortable or those who tire you."

The session with my daughter only takes ten minutes. I don't fully understand what happened at that moment. I observe that an incomparable happiness is present in her throughout the rest of our wonderful journey. A positive change has taken place. I can't help but make connections to her early childhood experiences as she "communicated" with lights. At that time, she was not able to share the information she received. I am pleased that circumstances have changed and that she is now able to do so.

It is with enthusiasm in the days that follow that I explore this new tool. I try the same technique first with my son and then with my husband. As soon as my hands come into contact with their bodies, something absolutely magical happens. It is as if their Higher Self is joining with mine. It is the reunion of our selves who have recognized each other for several lifetimes over hundreds of thousands of years. The energy emanating from my son also triggers the same phenomenon experienced with my daughter. A shimmering happiness and vibrant peace emanate from him. As far as my husband is concerned, the changes we have noticed are in our complicity and connection. A bond of communion, resulting from the fusion of our souls, has taken shape between us. Since then, we have been a whole.

I then contact Mary Rodwell about my profound experience, and she reassures me about the Language of the Stars. She explains that this language is universal, residing within everyone, though it mostly remains hidden.

That evening, I spend most of the night in a serene trance exploring aspects of myself that were previously unknown. Yes, everything is constantly in motion and the dimensions of oneself are constantly revealed! By placing my hands above me, I harness a powerful and electrifying energy that crisscrosses my body: I feel like I'm hovering in the atmosphere. Positioned next to me, I see my whole body as if it were a picture. It's a strange and fantastic feeling to be both present next to my body and lying in bed. My silhouette is transparent, like a delicate human shell. I can't move and my eyes remain closed. Yet, beneath the surface, a profound transformation is underway. A soft and almost inaudible language escapes from my mouth. My hand becomes an instrument. My fingers, which dance in the air, transmit codes of light. I'm elsewhere in another dimension while still being on the lookout for what's going on around me. It's a creative process. From this subtle procedure a new program is configured and implanted in myself. For about an hour, this procedure covers my entire body: the abdomen, then the legs, the neck and finally the eyes and head. This exercise is tiring. My hands and fingers hurt from the sustained effort. I feel like I've crossed the whole world in the space of those 60 minutes. Despite a wonderful feeling of rebirth, I succumb to a deep sleep that transports me to the first rays of the sun. When I wake up, serenity and a sense of accomplishment accompanies me to start the day. Plus, now, I'm bursting with vitality! Slight aches in the arm and hands are a concrete reminder of the transformation of the night. This nocturnal odyssey, guided only by my Higher Self, was a journey of self-healing.

This is only the opening act of a legendary discovery in my career. Each day that passes brings a notable evolution of my new abilities. Activated drop by drop, each session allows me to increase the power of my gifts. For two years, the learning, integration and ease of this tool were refined at night, first starting with myself. Witnessing the birth of my new skills, my husband regularly gets out of bed skillfully. He doesn't want to disturb me and above all, he wants to go to the couch so that he can sleep peacefully. The sessions on myself are not easy for him. I move the bed like a person who turns from one side to the other when sleep eludes them.

Chapter 16

A great secret well-hidden

Years after my gift was awakened in the Hawaiian Islands, I have an unexpected, pleasant encounter. Suddenly awakened from my sleep, I glance at the clock: three o'clock in the morning. As my eyes adjust to the dim light in the room, I'm surprised to see my paternal great-grandmother standing in front of me. I had not seen her since my childhood, not even at her funeral and not in my dreams either. She is identical to the image I have of her, that is to say the hair in a meticulous bun, a pale blue dress embellished with a beige silk collar and her sweet perfume that I loved so much.

I vividly remember the occasional moments I spent with her during her time on Earth. These meetings were particularly appreciated because they often took place during the holiday season. Her house, adorned with sumptuous Christmas decorations and filled with sweets, remains engraved in my memory. This woman faced adversity at a very young age. Part of her right arm was amputated after contracting polio. My father always knew his grandmother this way and had been told the same story. When I was a child, in no way did I consider her different from others. I have pleasant memories of her gently taking my hand and placing it on her severed arm, then covering it with her hand. Did she want me to feel her energy or to convey something meaningful to her?

Her visit that evening was short-lived. With her beautiful smile, she assures me that she will come back another time. At the same time the following night, she reappears. My great grandmother begins to tell the story of her last life on Earth...

— "Between the ages of five and eight, I experienced something unusual. This was around the early 1900s. My hand and sometimes even my body moved in strange and inexplicable ways. This was accompanied by strange sounds emanating from my mouth. These demonstrations continued and I began to stand out considerably from other little girls my age."

— "Our village, like many others in Quebec at that time, was a tight-knit community deeply rooted in religion. It goes without saying that the Church played a central role in our lives. Each person who sat in a pew at Mass was known not only by name, but also by their entire family history. My mother became more and more concerned about my behavior and the unusual words I was saying. Fearing the reaction of others when the strange events with me occurred, she resigned herself to asking for help. The parish priest was invited to our home in the hope that he will be able to give explanations on the phenomenon. As he watched me, as he listened to my mother's story, the priest immediately jumped to a shocking conclusion. According to him, I was under the influence of the devil! Out of fear, lack of knowledge and concern for my family's reputation and safety, he hurriedly consulted the village doctor. Together, the two men "of knowledge" discussed my case."

— "The ubiquitous gossip in the village held that I had become possessed by an evil force. It was claimed that this malevolent presence was harming me and even had the potential to spread and influence my brothers and sisters. Considering the perceived threat, the doctor recommended a drastic solution. I was told that the only way to thwart this sinister force that possessed me was to amputate my arm up to the elbow. They were really convinced that this was the only cure to drive the devil out of my body. They looked no further for the nature and effects of my unknown gestures and words."

— "Until the moment of amputation, prayers filled with hope begged for divine intervention or miraculous transformation. Unfortunately, nothing of the sort happened. The sacrifice of my perfectly healthy arm turned out to be completely useless. I carried a deep emotional scar and a permanent disability that turned the rest of my life upside down. In their vision of reality, the instrument through which "evil" was expressed had disappeared. From then on, I was out of danger and so were they. This disability is a painful reminder of the well-intentioned, but very misguided, actions taken by my family and the community."

— "This tragic event remained shrouded in silence. It was a taboo subject and became a hidden secret. It was buried inside me. It's a huge burden that I've carried for years without ever being able to share it. I have come to reveal the truth to you, dear Anick. I have come to tell you that you have inherited this gift. It is a legacy passed down from generation to generation. Our ancestors used it to heal and help many people. However, it is misunderstood, it has also brought them real suffering. Some have been brutally persecuted, others beaten, burned, and killed for exercising these special abilities. The pain is in the ink of the contract we voluntarily accepted before our earthly incarnations, designed to aid the evolution of humanity."

— "This gift has been entrusted to you to continue the work in your turn and it will be passed on to future generations. It has crossed the ages, waiting for the perfect moment to reveal itself. Its emergence in your life is timed to perfection. Of course, the method of burning at the stake no longer exists, but there were still some risks. The choice of the age of 43 is not random; it is your higher Self that decided before your incarnation. You deliberately postponed its demonstration until this stage to ensure your safety."

— "Not all members of our family necessarily understand the meaning of what I reveal to you. My dear child, the main thing is that you understand and appropriate this knowledge. Use this gift to heal your children, your husband, and those who place their faith in you. Negative influences will inevitably surround you, that's the nature of life. However, your happiness is paramount. Live with joy and fulfillment. We, the ancestors, need you now more than ever to continue the vital work of advancing humanity. By meeting and caring for people, you will sow seeds that will germinate in their own way and thus spread the richness that each one carries in the depths of his or her being. We love you and are always by your side. Never hesitate to call on us if you feel the need. I love you, Anick."

The sincere revelations I have just received astound me. I am shocked by the experiences of my father's grandmother. These messages bring me closer to my ancestor and forge a strong bond with this new additional ally. I am immensely grateful to her for entrusting me with this gift. I know what it's all about. I am determined to use it in the service of others. The explanations collected about my ability are reassuring!

I am very empathetic to the immense suffering that my great-grandmother endured. Of her eleven children, none of them have publicly expressed this gift. This is partly due to the hidden effects of their mother's trauma, including the fear that her offspring will suffer the same fate. The time was not conducive to this. Filled with compassion, my husband and children are sensitive to my pain at this tragic event, unlike the rest of my family. When I reveal this fact to them, my uncles and aunts refuse to accept and are still convinced that the amputation is due to polio. Their reality is quite different, and they do not question what is said about the past.

It is a moment like this that reminds us that we choose a family that stands in stark contrast to our own essence to explore the Earth. The role of family dynamics pushes us to transcend our predefined functions and to learn the things we have planned. My great-grandmother chose her parents, her time, and the moment of her reincarnation. She carried the weight of this pain to pave the way for future generations. What a great soul!

Chapter 17

My awakening to the Language of the Stars

With hindsight, I see how perfect the sequence of stages of my awakening are. All the orchestration of these manifestations on the Earth plane seems easy and natural in my pre-incarnation state. However, it is quite different when you have both feet on the ground!

The Language of the Stars, also known as "Light Language", has been dormant in me until the right moment. My guides told me that activating this gift earlier in my life would have been dangerous. There would have been risks to my health and safety due to the density of the third dimension. As I mentioned before, it is only at the age of 43 that I begin to develop this ability. I choose to call it "Le Langage des Étoiles" in French, although it could be defined differently.

As I deepen my practice, the initial mumblings start to make more sense, they have the power to change people's energy and frequencies, even if I don't quite understand the mechanisms behind it. My hand movements have become more focused and coordinated over the years. I realize that my gift is intertwined with other abilities.

Each of us have unique gifts, even if we do not use similar terms to describe them. The importance of using them for the betterment of humanity remains the basic rule. The term "Light Language" is somewhat diluted and overdone on social networks. It is for this reason that I have adopted a different term to better define my work.

The Language of the Stars is an inherent energy imprinted in oneself. It is made up of codes, words, sounds, gestures, and songs. It serves as a mode of communication through cosmic high frequency vibrations, decoded by our souls. This energy resides deep within the cells, and it can awaken memories within oneself. The activation of this language occurs when the individual is ready, as was the case for me in Hawaii. It's essential to remember that the power to improve our overall health and well-being lies within ourselves, our subconscious. The Language of the Stars supports the power of intention and self-healing to the extent that our words are aligned with our vibrations. Free will allows us to discern what is right and beneficial to ourselves.

Year after year, I have understood that there are as many Star Languages as there are different individuals in the universe. Just like on Earth where various languages and dialects are spoken. The difference is that these cosmic languages are understood by everyone. This universal form of language was forgotten or erased from our consciousness at birth. On the other hand, the Avatar children are familiar with this language. It's their vibration. They connect with this energy.

In ancient times, few children were born by caesarean section (C section). They went through their mother's gate. As a result, they acquired various knowledge and memories of their predecessors and parallel lives. This language is like a treasure waiting to be discovered. Our psychic can feel this spiritual awakening in the form of shivers and pulsations in our body. Now all children understand no matter what birth type.

If someone is not in resonance with a particular style of Language of the Stars, it means that they are not on the same vibrational frequency. During my Star Language sessions, I am lucky enough to be accompanied by the ancestors. They provide me with information that is crucial and helps entire lineages to free themselves from what has been hidden for a long time. Many of them died with well-kept secrets, often unspoken, or considered taboo. As long as they remain buried, they continue to affect us. This is transmitted to us and to our children in the form of blockage, discomfort, and illness. It is essential to discover and cure them to prevent them from being passed on to future generations. These messages are often enlightening, leading individuals to understand the source of their difficulties and sometimes causing noticeable changes in their lives. They prove to be truly liberating, not only for their personal growth, but also for the evolution of their entire lineage.

Chapter 18

My initiation

I allow myself all the time necessary to integrate the Language of the Stars. This tool will help to update my mission of helping others. By being more comfortable using it, I have the impetus to return to my meditation habits. The excitement of connecting to the spaceship is there. Day after day, it's a joy that I never get tired of!

One day, during a meditation, I overlook the Earth while waiting for the ship. When it arrives, emptiness and silence envelop the space when I enter. Intrigued, I continue on my way. I head to the children's section. The three Blue Beings and a Praying Mantis welcome me. They guide me through the white corridor. This square is impeccably clean, with a smell of disinfectant in the air. The feeling of coldness runs through my whole body while walking. Tenderness and immeasurable contentment take over and embrace me incredibly. Contrary to what I have experienced, it is not an easily definable feminine or masculine energy. Instead, I detect the unconditional compassion and love coming from my blue guides. The Mantis, which is like a galactic doctor, transmits serenity.

I arrive filled with emotions, but always accompanied at the end of the corridor in a medical-type room. The Praying Mantis signals me to stop; I listen to it. The image of the hologram of my mother lying in bed surrounded by Beings comes back to me. In a fraction of a second, I relive all the emotions related to my life here. I'm nostalgic for my classmates in other galaxies. What has happened to them? Where are they?

I quickly return to the present moment. I refocus my attention on my presence today... Who will I meet? What will my role be? Looking into the medical type of room, a young Blue Being turned gray black is lying on a bed. It's hard to ignore the immense sadness all around. I quickly understand that this Being is extremely ill. I have a strong desire to go and help him and demonstrate my usefulness in their world. So, I quickly walk towards him.

However, when I place my hands on the sick Being, panic engulfs me. The ego comes into play and I'm afraid I don't have the skills to heal it. A struggle takes place between my desire to be of service and the doubt of succeeding. In the midst of this emotional storm, something unexpected happens: the energies of the Blue Beings and the Praying Mantis merge harmoniously with mine. Instantly, this connection transforms me. My physical limitations dissolve and I become a conduit of healing energy. From my mouth and my hands, always placed above the little Being, come sounds and codes. When my hands rest on its chest, a soft blue light radiates and passes through the weakened body. I am amazed to see its vitality recover! I have the impression that knowledge filled with overflowing energy from ancient memories has been activated. The healed Being is transported to another room. They recognize my success and congratulate me. I see the impact of my actions and a sense of accomplishment draws a wide smile on my face.

This initiatory episode marks a pivotal moment in the use of my skills. I realize the effect of the combination of the energy of my hands, their movements, and the sounds I produce. The Language of the Stars is a medicine of the universe. We have only a fragment of an idea of its greatness and its possibilities.

A solid lesson

The contrast between the world of the Beings of Light and that of the Earth is a constant source of emotional turmoil for me. After this healing, I continue to float on a cloud of gratitude and love. The unconditional love experienced in this other dimension is truly rewarding. I feel valued and cherished. With all the impetus of this beautiful novelty, I put my mission back in the foreground. However, my concern increases when I think of the new generation of children. They arrive on Earth at this difficult moment in our evolution. People and children live by running. Many are detached from nourishing human values. In this case, it is complex to teach others how to live from oneself. My inner call is more powerful than ever. I am so keen to help and share the knowledge gained from the Beings of Light!

Despite my daily efforts and the sincere desire to reconnect, no contact is made. I literally feel abandoned. Nothing, complete silence! The Beings of Light no longer visit me. My wound of abandonment is an open wound. Desperate, I feed on the memories of what I experience when I am aboard the ship: I forget that I am human and the time spent on board is intangible, slipping through my fingers like the finest grains of sand. Earthly concerns and emotions seem insignificant to me. I feel like I have increased my abilities tenfold. In my thoughts, my dreams or in meditation, the same feeling of abandonment arises when, as a child, I had to cross a rigid white cylinder to return to Earth. In this elongated tube, which has become denser and tighter, I have difficulty breathing. Sad, isolated, neglected once again. I'm completely disoriented. But what have I done? I miss my cosmic family terribly. In attempting to rekindle this cosmic connection, I am inadvertently abandoning my responsibilities and my loved ones. Time passes and I have had no news for almost three months. By losing my daily close contact with the spaceship, I increase my daily contact with my family. I have no choice but to be more present in the human dimension. As a result of this realization, I receive the reason for their absence by a download in a dream. They made me realize that my unwavering commitment to them led me to abandon my family, my kids, my husband, and my faithful dog. In addition, I did not realize the extent of the isolation I imposed on myself.

I'm lucky to be able to walk between the two realities. That's my strength. It is up to me to actualize it here below instead of perfecting it above. The lesson was painful to digest. Life demands a harmonious balance. My presence is required in the world I inhabit, just as I am needed in other realms. It is with humility that I accept to accommodate the different spheres of my life. My goal is to find ways to reach people and children of the new generation to support them in the healing of certain ailments and to advise them.

The electricity in our body

While on vacation in charming Vancouver Island, Canada, in the middle of a full moon night, I wake up inhabited by a powerful Star Language. It makes my fingers move with a speed never seen before and the codes follow one another in sounds in the aforementioned way. An electricity enters my body, passes through it, and makes my fingers sparkle. This phenomenon has been happening more frequently since the beginning of my vacation. I am careful not to disturb my husband who is sleeping next to me. In the early morning, I receive new details about my gift of language. My guides tell me that they have made an update. It enhances my ability to support humans in making the transition to the new dimension. As they take pleasure in reminding me, I chose this precise moment to receive this particular activation.

Through my Star Language, I am able to release energy that can transmit electricity. This transmission can be to another person, animal, plant, food and/or water. In fact, everything is made up of electricity and energy. In this context, this is determined by the inner vibration present in everything: water, living food, nature, sounds, colors, emotions, and love. The harmonious interaction between electricity and these vital elements is essential to our health. An insufficiency of these constituents or excessive acidity in the body will create an imbalance. This will disrupt the flow of internal electricity and can lead to illness.

My role is to act as a catalyst, to activate and amplify this internal electricity in the body. However, this work of transformation does not occur alone. To improve the electrical load, it is imperative that the person takes responsibility for their balance. It seems obvious to say it, but incorporating a sensible lifestyle is key. In addition to everything you already know about getting enough sleep, regular physical activity, and eating a healthy diet, I add the following components: being in love with yourself and existence as well as connecting with the Earth. Neglecting this connection causes us to weaken little by little. Our system is less and less effective. Also, when we're not at our best, we tend to crave foods that harm us. Therefore, it is essential to take care of ourselves with kindness without falling into excesses.

To thrive, we need to be in harmony with our environment and with each other. The connections we make contribute to the transfer of electricity in this vast interconnected network of life. Duality no longer has its place: blessings are complementary to lessons; lessons are complementary to the blessings. It is in this space that another facet of the grandeur and beauty of life is revealed to us.

Personally, I feel immense satisfaction when I transfer my energy to another human, animal, or plant. To harmonize with this new dimension we are entering, our body needs to be optimized or recalibrated. During a Star Language session, this is exactly what happens. Energy is transferred to the other person through my hands and body, resetting and reconnecting their inner power grid.

In the City of Light, each inhabitant can access electricity or light according to their needs. The electricity generated by their bodies activates the illumination of this City. There are no wires or technology; Everything flows seamlessly. The beings who live there have the ability to restart, repair or rewire their internal electrical network. In fact, many other people on Earth are connected to it. This ubiquitous electricity has earned it the name "City of Light". I now understand the meaning of the first appearance of the City connected to the river by a flash of lightning when I was fifteen years old!

The reason many are unable to perceive it is because it is behind the veil of third-dimensional reality. Our eyes have been conditioned not to see energy. My Beings of Light have mentioned that our vision is evolving to adapt to this new dimension. It is common for people to find that they no longer need glasses as their perceptions change. The more we become aware of the invisible, the more we develop our gifts, the more energetic strength we acquire. The more our inner power grows and solidifies, the less we leave it to others. And it is in this vibratory state that we become sovereign.

Exposing myself to the Light

I continue to perfect my gift by practicing on my own family members. Having already experimented with my children and my husband, I turn to my mother and my relatives. It's not an easy path. I had to face an inevitable obstacle, disbelief. Those around me have a hard time grasping the scope of the healing potential. I help people overcome deep-rooted emotional wounds that usually cause long-standing health problems.

Despite my proven ability to help heal emotional disorders, my extended family finds it difficult to trust me. Especially when it comes to their children. They don't understand the value of my services, seeing them as intangible and questionable compared to conventional medicine. Revealing your gifts and abilities to your loved ones can be a complex and demanding process. The harshest criticism comes from them. The desire to help and heal my loved ones is sincere, but I commonly encounter resistance. I therefore made the decision to stop offering my services to them. Yet, I remained steadfast in my commitment to accomplish my mission on Earth. Other people can benefit from what I have to offer.

In my early days, the Star Language sessions were done with my close friends who volunteered. I offer a lot of sessions for free, considering myself an apprentice. Each session is a valuable learning opportunity. Every client encounter is different. Although the process remains similar, they enrich my connection to the spiritual world. By word of mouth, a clientele not only in my hometown, but also from all over the world, began to grow. My reputation for perceiving the afterlife, hearing, sensing, and interacting in unique ways with the presence of the deceased attracts people from all over the world. They ask me for advice, intrigued by the promise of connecting with their ancestors.

In 2016, I was approached to give a talk about my special experiences and the Language of the Stars. My first reaction is to doubt, fearing that no one will believe my story, because it seems to come straight out of a science fiction movie. However, I recognize the call to open up more and make myself known to a wider audience in order to help as many people as possible. It is with nervousness and determination that I accept the invitation. In a two-hour lecture, I explain how my gift was activated and how I use it for the greater good of all. To my surprise and delight, the audience highly appreciated the presentation. Nearly 100 people listened attentively, captivated by the story of my life. The positive reception of the assembly reassures my insecurity. It's good for the human in me! I feel on the right track knowing that I am touching and changing people's lives.

In the fall, I have the opportunity to be interviewed by Jean Casault, one of Canada's most renowned ufologists. He is a man I hold in high regard, considering him a mentor. I believe he spent time on one of the spaceships as a commander. He becomes a central figure in my life. He is a mentor who guides me and encourages me to be discovered. His influence and guidance supported me in my first steps. As a result of this transformative interview, my sessions took on a new dimension. Public speaking dissolves resistance from doubt and fear. Something has definitely manifested itself inside of me: a new confidence that allows me to be intensely connected to my mission in a functional way. As a result, I am attracting more and more customers. People contact me on the recommendation of those who have experienced the benefits of my sessions.

Invitations to other interviews and conferences began to pour in. Hence, I have the opportunity to present my story to a wider audience and larger gatherings. The positive feedback encourages me to continue. I continue to evolve and remain authentic more easily. I am at peace with this spiritual agreement that I have signed that is being fulfilled at this point in my life. When the path becomes irreversible, all we have to do is go ahead and look for everything we need to move in the new direction.

Our spirit guides willingly put us to the test when we reach this point of self-discovery and embrace our mission. The impact of coming out of my shell extended beyond my own person. My children and my husband, already open to the most mystical aspects of my being, have benefited from it. My spouse benefited from the gifts I was able to give him, both personally and professionally on the financial side. I offer him advice, I suggest directions and alternatives so that he remains true to himself, to his Light.

A dear wish fulfilled

In the middle of my "normal" life, I continue to visit the spaceship in search of answers in an effort to improve myself. In one of my trips, when I walk through a long white tunnel, each step reveals shapes and silhouettes accompanied by subtle vibrations. As I move further, nature and animals appear in front of me. I recognize a presence that cuddles me. It is a radiant feminine energy, filled with warmth and beauty. She's my daughter! The joy of her presence fills my heart. It's a moment I've been dreaming about countless times. Moving a little further, I meet another vibration that I recognize without any hesitation: it's my son! His presence is still linked to the technology section. This time, he deals with the circulation of civilizations and distances. I feel a fulfillment and a great unity that can be found in several dimensions. I wonder if my husband is also present. I always suspected that he has a role to play in this cosmic mission. With a deep breath, I let the air fill my lungs. Suddenly, I pick up on his distinct vibration. To my surprise, there is no physical form of him here, only a hologram that appeared in front of me. I reach out to touch the hologram. Even though he lacks substance, I can feel his presence through its vaporous form. Knowing where he is intrigues me. I wonder why he's not in the spaceship. It is the Beings of Light who provide me with an answer: he is not on any space fleet. My husband is at the control tower, overseeing the movement of ships in this galaxy. I am relieved to be informed that he is with us and that he is carrying out his mission with dedication and determination. His role is related to the governance of ships in the cosmos. I'm euphoric! The four of us are together in this dimension.

Chapter 19

The non-time

My meditation journeys have always taken me to places where the vibration allows me to offer essential help to those in need. On this day, I am transported to a country and a time similar to the early 1900s. The style of the dwellings and amenities evokes images from the Titanic era. What is remarkable this time is the fact that I am not destabilized by my environment. My consciousness is aligned with my soul. It's as if it were natural to witness such a spectacle.

I find myself in a city, then in a house and finally in the room of a terribly sick and suffering child. This reminds me of the time I healed the little girl in my other meditation. As I scan the room, I see the spirits of her ancestors standing near the bed. The ethereal beings are impatiently waiting for the deliverance of the girl. They are meant to be comforting her. The suffering will end, and everything will be for the best. Meanwhile, around her, parents and family are overwhelmed by tears. Overwhelmed by their powerlessness in the situation, they are gathered around her, accompanying her until her last breath.

Standing in front of this child, I see that the thread that connects her soul to her body is about to break. I communicate with her telepathically. She can no longer stand the suffering and shares with me her strong desire to escape her pain. She is also tormented by the worries and grief of her family. I reassure her by gently repeating that things will get better. She can leave. There is no need to put up with more. It is then that a girl of the same age dressed in a sari appears next to the bed. She stands there, analyzing the almost empty body in front of her. Her gaze wanders between the sick child and me. She waits. I don't comprehend her visit. The ancestors present do not give me any details. As soon as I gently put my hands on her body, I feel an energy flowing inside the dying child. As I focus on her, her identity dissolves. I observe a strange black smoke escaping from her body. The soul of the girl detaches from her fragile body. I am saddened. I am unable to help her. The child dressed in an Indian garment telepathically says to me:

— "In the life I just left, nothing was happening to develop what I had to accomplish. That's why I died. However, it was a time when the way of life was easier. That era is very close to yours, by the way. I came to join the body of this soul that has just left because we have an agreement. Her soul contract is over. She has no choice but to leave. It was agreed between the two of us that I would take back her body to continue my life here. I will be able to be who I am and do my mission, even if it is a moment "spent" in the timeline of the Earth."

Seconds after finishing her sentence, an inexplicable force gently sucks her into a vortex. The girl dressed in a sari disappears, easily integrating the deserted body. After a short while, the frail body begins to regain color and tone. A deep and invigorating breath escapes from the girl... Unaware of what has just happened in the energy, the loved ones are flabbergasted to see what is happening before their eyes. Filled with gratitude, they repeat with tears of relief that a miracle has just happened.

When I return from my meditation, I am shaken and confused. A scene of this magnitude unfolded before my eyes for a reason. I wondered if I had traveled back in time. Usually, I go to other dimensions. It is an event that seems inconceivable to me. According to the young Indian woman's explanations, it is quite common. This leads me to think about the fluidity of time and existence, the interaction between the past, the present and the future. I am also reorienting my understanding of our multidimensional aspect. This thought occupied my thoughts for years. Through this child's teaching, I learned to differentiate between "time does not exist" and non-time. Rather, the concept of timelines is redefined by opportunities to experience, realize, and achieve oneself continuously without relying on the past, present or future.

It's quite a revelation for me. I have just discovered that I do not only use energy to heal, but also to help the transfer of souls into a body. Indeed, it is one of the many possibilities of the unlimited functioning of energy that our soul knows. Forgotten, this ability is neglected in favor of traditional medicine. Comforting, healing, seeing the afterlife, supporting passages, and integrating into a body are strengths that we all possess. I am not the only one destined to accompany in this way. This ability is present in our DNA in a dormant state for the majority of people. Please be aware, however, that we may choose to access it.

Imagine in front of you a very thick book filled with thin pages. Each page represents one of your lives. The book holds within it all your past, present and future lives in this dimension and the others. The pencil is you. Now you just have to run the pencil through the pages to begin to capture the full essence of your soul's experience. Your entire self.

Chapter 20

Change in perception

The moment I gave birth to my twins, a huge realization arrived. The two beings who shared great moments in the school on the spaceship with me are in fact my own children in this life. Our lives have unfolded in parallel, and each of these events has occurred simultaneously across the lifelines of existence. While we are taught to perceive time in a linear way, the higher dimensions reveal that all these lives exist simultaneously. The meeting with my children on the spaceship coincides with the time of their coming into the world as my descendants. It is a fusion of the "past" and the present. As I explore the timeless intertwined bonds of our souls, I understand that our mission together has been stretching since the dawn of time! The concept of time, as I have known it since the beginning of my human life, is unraveling. I realize that I can revisit the ship and relive what happened any time.

My experiences, coupled with a client's anecdote, lead me to make the following deduction: what we may find repulsive on Earth usually corresponds to the missions we voluntarily undertake elsewhere. During a session, the client confides in me that she had worked in the "room as I describe with dolls" in the spaceship. In her vision, she is in an immaculate white room with several babies. She tenderly takes one of the babies and holds it close to her. A warmth of love and bliss is exchanged between them. The vibration of this shared energy is inscribed in her whole being. However, in her life on Earth, she does not consider herself particularly maternal by nature. This woman does not feel the urge to take care of babies with enthusiasm, as she experiences during her night trips.

The contrast is striking between our earthly self and the roles we play across borders. In the reality of parallel lives, anything is possible. We can be ourselves, occupying various roles while embodying some of our ancestors or an individual of our descendants. The presence of the many hybrid beings living among us adds to all this. It is plausible that we, our children and/or our grandchildren have a connection to each other's mission. This concept is abstract and there is no point in forcing it to the forefront of our consciousness. There is no need to turn your life upside down by looking for answers at all costs. This way of perceiving may or may not be included in your reality. Embrace the idea that it is not the sum of theories and knowledge that is most important; It is the feeling and what resonates with you when this knowledge comes to you. Everything is perfect, no matter how much information you remember. You've come to the right place at the right time.

Our Earth is undergoing major transformations. What I experienced at the age of six is spreading more and more among the new generation of children. This leads me to frequently inform my clients that their children can embody the wisdom of their ancestors. These young souls chose their parents for one reason: to pass on valuable teachings.

Chapter 21

Visitors are among us

Like many, vacations give me a respite from the burden of everyday life. The more I relax, the more receptive I am to the wisdom contained in the guidance of my Beings of Light. My understanding of the teachings received in my dreams and meditations improve.

A fabulous encounter took place on a camping trip in the Alberta Rocky Mountains in Canada in July 2017. Our family had set up camp on serene land directly in front of the majestic mountains. In a peaceful sleep, around 2 a.m., I ventured out of the tent to go to the washroom. I take the opportunity to contemplate the starry expanse above my head for a few moments. Suddenly, the sky changes. My gaze is drawn to the mountain behind me which seems to be splitting. Large beams of intensely radiant white light emerge from this space. It's an extraordinary sight that makes my heartbeat with excitement. Two swaying figures gradually stand out in the center. These figures seem to invite me silently. Beneath my amazement, a small fear remains. Above the summit, I notice that the sky reveals something else: a giant gray shape, tinged with azure, suspended in the middle of the heavens. The breach in the mountain is like an entrance and exit leading to something bigger. Could it be a spaceship?

I recognize the energy of otherworldly beings. My breathing accelerates. My sense of connection is as deep as when I am in other dimensions through meditation. Information presents itself to me like a flowing river. I realize that once again, I have the chance to experience an improbable event. But why me? And why now?

I close my eyes. I lose all sense of time and space. Everything flows in a way detached from the world. When I open my eyes again, there is nothing left. Everything has vanished. In the dark web of the sky, only the thin line that forms the perimeter of the mountain remains. The night mist settles on my skin and face. My body shivers from the moisture that had seeped into my bones. I return to my tent to find the warmth and comforting presence of my husband. As sleep overtakes me, a question comes up. Is it possible that these enigmatic beings from another dimension are on Earth with the intention of living among us?

I wake up a little disoriented at dawn. My experience of the mountains fades to look more like a dream. When planning our day, an impulse pushes me to head to a famous lake called, Lake Louise, located in the forest about 40 minutes from our camp. Despite our original plans, my husband and children agreed without hesitation to change the itinerary for the day. Upon arrival, I had a keen intuition that something unique was waiting to be discovered. How lucky are we to find that on this morning, the lake is deserted by tourists! I ask my husband to watch over the children for a few moments. He nods in agreement, and I venture to a lonely rock not far from the shore. Resting on the stone, I close my eyes for an inner journey. I return to my meditative trance state. In this state of tranquility, I reach a realm that I don't quite remember.

When I open my eyes, an uncomfortable realization presses on me. I feel like I've been away for an hour or more. I hurry to join my husband and children.

— "I'm sorry, I didn't realize how long I was gone."

— "Don't worry, my love, it's only been ten minutes."

The distortion of time and space puzzled me. However, meditation always refreshes my mind. Then suddenly my gaze is drawn to the mountains before me.

Resembling a hologram, a transparent bridge of light suspended between the two mountains gradually appears. I frown and close my eyes, assuming it's an illusion. When I look again, the bridge continues to shine in broad daylight. My vision is beyond comprehension. My heart is pounding. My intuition was right.

I wonder if at the end of this bridge is the same City of Light that I have seen many times during my travels. I see people crossing the luminous bridge. I recognize my husband, my children and even our dog walking there. Their appearance is a few years older. My being is permeated by a vibration different from the one I feel on Earth. Curious, I turn to my husband and children who are by my side. I ask them if they see the same thing, hoping that the children share my reality. They usually perceive the subtleties of the world with wonder and candor. Their bright eyes find the show magical, as if they were witnessing a captivating fairy tale. My husband sees nothing and feels nothing. He observes the children running in their illusion and in their imagination. My son explains to me that it reminds him of a dream he has repeatedly: he sees a mountain opening up. Lasers come out of the same place and envelop the Beings who put on a "human uniform". Later, by pure chance, he reveals to me that this mountain that he dreams of is located in Australia: it is the mountain of Uluru. Nevertheless, my vision is confirmed by a dream visit the following night:

— "You've seen how we move. The mountain opens up, allowing our energy to flow in and out. In a way, the mountains serve as our home."

In the days following our return home, I do a session with a client. During this session, my work immerses me in the role of a channeler for the Beings of Light. They turn my attention back to the bridge seen at Lake Louise. I am informed that they are unfortunately forced to change their location. The increasing influx of tourists has made the energy too dense for them. More information will be disclosed to me later when the time is right.

A few days later, with another client, the course of the session takes a strange turn. The man addresses me telepathically in disclosing some information. Clearly, this person was chosen for this session with me at this time. He served as a channeler to give me a glimpse of my future. I am infinitely grateful for this intense exchange. In return, I offered him a free session in the image of the generosity of his heart. Since his session became mine. As soon as the client left, I went outside to enjoy the sun, purify myself and recharge my batteries. I ask myself: was this customer a Visitor? During my relaxation, I once again become a channeler. Additional information comes to me from the Mountain Beings. Memories resurface one by one. They identified themselves as the "Visitors" and revealed their purpose:

⏤ "We are here, Anick, to visit your planet, to experience human life, for your progress and ours. Few people are aware of our presence. Yet, we have left our marks for hundreds of years to signal our existence."

Chapter 22

An unexpected revelation

This occurrence takes place in December 2021. We are now residing in Ecuador in a quiet little fishing village named Crucita. While waiting for our new home in the Andes, we are staying in a condominium building on the beach. It contains ten apartments. Ours is located on the beachfront and offers the best ocean views. At the moment, there is only one other condominium occupied and it is an elderly lady and her small dog who live there.

It's a night that begins like any other, when at around 10:30 p.m. an exceptionally high-pitched noise disturbs our sleep. The sound, unlike anything we've heard before, seems to come from the stairwell in the entryway. Surprised, curious, and attracted by the noise, my husband and I get out of bed. When we open the door, we notice that the strange tone comes straight out of the old lady's apartment, just above ours. Total surprise: the noise stops almost as suddenly as it started. Disconcerted, I close the door. The noise resumes immediately. This little merry-go-round repeats itself: every time our door is open, the noise stops instantly, and when we close it, the sound resonates throughout the building again.

It is laborious to describe what we hear. One could compare the sound to the effect of the amplified song of a thousand locusts. This dissonant concert sends shivers down our spines. It continues intermittently throughout the night. We don't dare approach her apartment. Strangely, her dog remained silent, as it is normally very vocal. The situation leaves us insomniac and disturbed until the first light of the morning. Worried about the elderly lady's well-being, I contacted her daughter, whom we had already met a few times. I tell her about our concerns about the strange sounds coming from her mother's apartment. Her answer reassures us, because she says that everything is in order and that everything is fine with her mom and the dog. However, our peace is short-lived. In the night, around one o'clock in the morning, the incomparable and disturbing noise wakes us up again from sleep. Coming from the same apartment, it resounds once again throughout the stairwell. Determined to find out what it's all about, this time we try to get closer. At the moment when we open the door, the noise ceases again immediately.

It is at this point that a question arises: what if these inexplicable sounds were generated by intelligent Beings from another dimension? Do they have the ability to detect our vibrations and is this what causes them to stop their activities every time they feel our presence?

With a slight concern, I suggest my husband to venture upstairs. With a video camera on his mobile phone, he will try to document the strange event. Leaving our apartment, we close the door as if we had gone inside. The shrill sound resumes, a sign that our plan is working. With his heart pounding and sweaty palms, my husband carefully climbs the few steps leading directly to the door where this strange piercing sound came from. Determined, he approaches quietly. The camera registers an intense white light that is a little bluish, under the threshold of the door. Intermittently, it picks up on the presence of shapeless black shadows. Climbing two or three steps to pass the door to the top floor, everything stops suddenly. His presence has surely been detected. It is in complete silence that my husband comes down to me. With a frightened face and at the same time proud, he hands me the phone. Speechless and always on the alert, we watch together the short videos containing the evidence of what we cannot explain. The videos captured allow us to take a step back and confirm that it is a phenomenon from another reality. A good two hours pass before we can sleep again. Fortunately, all this time, our children remain perfectly asleep while dreaming peacefully.

Before continuing my night, the need to meditate comes up. I am looking for answers and I believe that connecting with my stellar family is the best way to find them, understand, and most importantly comfort myself. Once settled, I begin the meditation stages. Spontaneously, I express myself in a celestial and starry language. The energy in the room changes immediately. An unidentifiable presence approaches me. Although my husband is asleep next to me, I feel a certain uneasiness. I hesitate to open my eyes as if I fear that I will encounter something terrifying again. The night is a playground where mysterious forces take on more importance in our human environment. Well concentrated, I maintain my meditative state with my eyes closed. I can feel positive invisible presences. My hand, apparently guided by an external force, begins to move on its own. It would seem that it is to establish a form of communication. I am receptive to incoming information from these curious Beings who present themselves as "Visitors of Light". Their message unfolds in a telepathic exchange without images.

⸺ "We have temporarily taken up residence in this apartment. Everything was methodically planned. We chose this place to blend in perfectly with the environment. Thus, we can go unnoticed. This apartment is an ideal strategic point for us to move freely to and from the ocean. It is a bridge between dimensions. Our means of communication go beyond your language and your human senses. We converse through the Language of the Stars, transferring energy and knowledge between us. The sounds that seem irritating to you are simply the manifestations of our discussions."

These Beings have found that I have received information concerning their existence and visit.

⸺ "There are no coincidences, as you proclaim. Just three days before we arrived, you were writing about our presence and mission on Earth. Now you have concrete evidence of our existence here on Earth. In addition, the fact that you remember our encounters and use your knowledge is of essential meaning to us. The work you will initiate, Anick, is of immense importance. It is now your duty to share this experience with those who need to be awakened. Many will be doubtful.

The most important thing is that you now have undeniable evidence of our presence among you."

This interview with them completely changed the nature of what my husband and I have just experienced. From a troubling enigma, it turns into a collaboration, even a mandate. This complements the work already undertaken in my mission. The Being continues his message by giving more details about their process:

— "I am a Visitor. When I arrived, I underwent a major transformation. Originally, I manifest in the form of light. I then take on a human appearance. So, I'm naked when I arrive. A bag of clothes is left in a specific place provided by advanced technological tools. Our first action is to get this bag! We must adapt to our bodies. It is our vessel to move and experience. Just like you, in fact. In addition to the instructions received, snippets of information that you call memories come to us. These downloads are crucial to living, reacting, and functioning in our new environment. We don't go through the same developmental milestones that you go through in your life here. We are not humans."

— "Everything is orchestrated down to the last detail. Our representative is notified of our arrival and receives instructions. Its role is to provide essential information about the way of life here, to locate the nearest portals and dimensions that serve as emergency exits in case of need."

— "Hosts are individuals who were once Visitors like me. They decided to make the Earth their permanent home. They volunteer to welcome newcomers and facilitate their integration into the human population. Although we arrive in an invisible state, our particular frequencies are felt by some sentient beings. It is for this reason that, more often than not, this meeting point is a vast space hidden from human perception. We arrive during the night. The preferred places are deep in forests, deserts, oceans, and quiet shores. Our representative introduces us to the basic rules of human life. Using visual aids, we learn how to use amenities, furniture, and accessories. We have to integrate the norms governing sleep, mealtimes and food appreciation. Already valid identification documents such as birth certificates and passports are given to us. It is at this moment that we appropriate our first and last names on Earth. The art of creating these documents is a well-established practice among the Visitors who reside on Earth. It is easy to produce all the material necessary to blend in with the crowd, given our assimilation into diversified strategic roles. We are present in all sectors of your professions: natural resources, industries, business, science, research, law, health, education, food, tourism, government, etc."

⊢ "The first moments after their arrival are destabilizing. They have to manage a multitude of protocols in order to be able to act in a similar way to humans. Once settled, the more Visitors are involved in welcoming newcomers, the more they are rewarded in highly prized areas: human interactions and emotions. Human conversation is complicated for them. They receive downloads that enhance the ease of their social interactions. Understanding emotions is also facilitated and propelled. The terms of their contract here prevent them from functioning telepathically."

⊢ "Over time, the Visitors adapt to life on Earth. Their Light energy gradually dissipates during their "transformation" towards the human they embody. They never refer to their non-human origins when talking about themselves. In this way, they experience and fully learn what it is like to be human and to live on the planet. Interactions have a slightly awkward, but dynamic tendency with us. Children and some adolescents have the ability to perceive the origin of this lack of skills."

Like many others, my son is inclined to recognize the presence of these type of individuals. Usually, everything fades away around the age of twelve, unless the living environment encourages these skills. Compared to the energy capacities of animals, plants and beings outside the Earth, humans are unfortunately the least developed.

The prospect of sharing this stunning unexpected revelation with the world worries me. I concede that the truth will be met with skepticism, criticism, and judgment. However, it has the potential to inspire real change through awakening, openness, and the realization that we are part of a whole greater than we can imagine. And that's exactly what humanity needs!

When I return from this surprising meditation, I take the time to integrate all of this information.

Chapter 23

Our side mission

I'll take you back to 2015. During our family sabbatical, my husband and I took a vacation, leaving our children in the care of my parents. Visiting the Ecuadorian coastal region, we explored several fishing villages. One place in particular stood out to me. Popular and crowded, yet the village of Crucita seemed to me that it was not properly taken care of. It was not a place I would want to settle in. In addition to the disappointing visual observation, I couldn't figure out what bothered me. I told my husband that we would never go back again... In the months that followed, I had the same dream over and over again: I was underwater in the ocean, and I was somehow breathing. I was coming back to the surface, with only my eyes at sea level looking at the beach in the distance. In this dream, my husband and children were always present by my side. When I woke up, I felt like I was leaving a place I knew well, in which every member of the family played a role. I saw them busy with tasks that required great concentration. However, I didn't know what the purpose of this teamwork was. My role was to manage everything including other specific tasks that were also assigned to me. The meaning of this dream remained a complete mystery for a very long time. The repetition of this scenario led me to believe that I was possibly on a very important mission, but no confirmation to that effect reached me.

Circumstances made our whole family stay in Crucita in late 2021, waiting for the availability of our house to start our new life in Ecuador. An unimaginable unveiling marks this occasion. After the initial meeting with the Visitors, further information came to me in the form of powerful energetic exchanges with them. This time, it wasn't just about me. The lives of each of my family members were concerned. I was taught and explained that this village was a point of attachment for two parallel lives among many others. We had just completed a momentous mission for humanity in another dimension. I must admit that I was confused. The very vivid memories of my experience were called into question. I resisted these confusing disclosures for quite some time.

From 2015 to 2021, we were all living simultaneously in Calgary, Canada and at an underwater base off the coast of Crucita. My brain has a lot of difficulty absorbing the explanations of the Visiting Beings and my Beings of Light. Our routine of life in Calgary was actually an illusion, a manifestation that we had created. How is this possible? Every morning, I would make breakfast for my children before driving them to school and my husband would go to work. Everything was physically tangible! The Beings specified that when leaving the house, our environment was activated gradually by our intention: roads, buildings, cityscape, etc. As far as I was concerned, I was already in other dimensions by channeling the Language of the Stars during the sessions with clients. However, I did not perceive the alternative life of seven years in which my involvement was revealed. Coexisting in two different realities is a concept that takes a moment to integrate into my understanding. It makes you wonder if everything you are experiencing is true or only multiple illusions!

The Higher Beings told me that it all started in 2015 when I visited Crucita with my husband. That was the beginning of our mission. They pointed out again that during our lives in Calgary, we had never really left the confines of the underwater base. Every member of my family played a crucial role in a prime project that had a major impact. Our mission was centered on an interdimensional portal designed to receive and transmit new energy to entities and Beings from various galaxies who wished to come to Earth.

This workstation was equipped with advanced technology that is reminiscent of CERN[5]'s innovations, and HAARP[6] in their research efforts. The base itself was a spherical structure. Inside, there was a black and navy-blue hole. It served as a gateway to a multitude of different realities, connecting our planet to other worlds, dimensions, and timelines. It had facilitated the movement of beings, objects, animals, and even elemental forces (air, water, earth, and fire). This construction was not ordinary. As a result, it has piqued the curiosity of Beings from several distant galaxies. All kinds of forms of entities and energies could try to pass through.

In the underwater base, we were part of a team responsible for welcoming and supervising Beings arriving from other galaxies. The previous team did not have the training or knowledge to effectively manage and regulate entities accessing the portal. As a result, an influx of negative entities had access to it until 2015. When we arrived, my husband, children, and I were tasked with assessing and redirecting everything that came through the portal. We filtered out the malevolent entities such that they did not affect the positive Beings who came to help humanity. This responsibility alone demonstrates the importance of our mission. It was a complex environment. Each member of the family played an exclusive role in this security mandate. Our expertise was interdependent. They complemented each other. In this crucial work, our collective survival depended on everyone's accuracy. Entities approaching the portal were often motivated by curiosity and adventure. Among these, several had a much less noble intention than discovery, such as espionage. Using dubious pretexts, their presence posed a real threat, as they aimed to upset the balance of our planet by causing destruction. Thanks to the detectors in the first stage, we effectively

---

[5] European Council for Nuclear Research based in Switzerland, an intergovernmental organization that operates the world's largest particle physics laboratory including testing around with dark matter which can displace Earth's geomagnetic field lines.
[6] High-Frequency Active Auroral Research Program, an Alaska-based center where the ionosphere is studied.

intercept this kind of danger. As sentinels of this gateway to the Earth, we ensured that only what helps humanity could cross. It was an arduous, somewhat daunting responsibility.

Working as a family made this experience an exclusive one. Although they were only seven years old at the time, our children had a prenatal contract to help us in our mission. It is the mature souls who inhabit them who have contributed to the realization of this task.

My husband's role was of paramount importance. He was responsible for overseeing the integrity of realities and ensuring the stability of the portal. He was monitoring the latter's filter. He meticulously measured the concordance of each fraction of a second, the vibrations and energy that flowed through it. He had to calculate very accurately in order to avoid or minimize the potential disasters that could occur if these separate existences touched. Such cataclysms could manifest themselves in the form of earthquakes or tsunamis in the places concerned. We know their disastrous and unfortunate consequences.

My son's exclusive task was both intriguing and challenging. Resilience was one of his great strengths. He was associated with a team of spider-like Beings. It was a collaboration that had a certain irony since he has a fear of these creatures in his earthly life. In this alternate dimension, he served as an engineer. He was responsible for building and maintaining a complex spider web that covered the energy sphere. With his team, he ensured the robustness of the mesh. His daily responsibilities included calculating, repairing, observing, and maintaining the canvas, which was itself composed of a canvas, in its interior. This armor was subject to disturbances caused by external forces from entities. Needless to say, this protection was essential.

My daughter held a function directly related to the balance between terrestrial interactions and galactic explorers. With her special ability, she absorbed and purified everything that entered our world through the portal. Everything that passed through the portal had to undergo a transformation to adapt to Earth's conditions. She assiduously awaited the arrival of Beings, vegetation, animals, insects and even the elements. She also modified creatures in other universes that were too scary or incompatible with life on Earth.

After this initial purification of being attuned to the energies of the Earth, the travelers were sent to the City of Light. The goal was to reprogram their DNA. Without this stay, the balance on the planet would have been compromised because of the many infections that would have spread. Once all the steps of the process were completed, the travelers integrated into the ecosystem of our planet.

As for me, my responsibilities were oriented towards assisting beings in need of care. This passage is extremely trying. Some do not survive. The entities have one last chance to regain their health, otherwise they would be recycled back into the universe. Moreover, they dissipated to another dimension or a parallel life. I channeled light energy to rebuild their DNA program. I provided guidance through vibrational communication and touch. I used my Star Language to make connections and create a welcoming environment for them. My task was accomplished when those who were too fragile left or when the healing was complete, and they were able to live in our world. The transformation was so demanding that some beings could not raise their vibrations, even with all my care. For the others, due to changes in their bodies and frequencies, the changes in their structure were irreversible. No return to their original origin was conceivable. The only way to leave was to experience the passage of death.

Once the purification and transformation steps were successful, travelers were required to pass through a City of Light. It was specifically designed to assess their compatibility with Earth's conditions. This stopover was an illusion for them. They had no memory of it. The duration of this internship was considerable. The survivors of the portal came to Earth because they were attracted to its energy. They have to adapt themselves to its functioning. Upon successful completion of the training, they were assigned a representative to oversee their behavior on the planet. The reason for their presence is different from the Visitors who have the mandate to experience life on earth with a humanitarian mission.

Looking back and thinking carefully, there were several signs of our life in Calgary that confirmed the existence of our parallel mission. The fears, passions and current strengths of my children, my husband and I are directly related to the functions we held in the submarine station.

In short, I understood that we are constantly living parallel lifelines and that, in general, we are able to recognize only one: that of the here and now. For some, experiencing one or more parallel lives is natural. Without really knowing it, we sail and cross several of them simultaneously. The guides share ways to open up and become more aware of this concept. It is a question of observing and interpreting our lives and what makes up our being in this incarnation in a different way. For example, what characterizes us in this incarnation (our personality, our dislikes, our talents, our interests, our aspirations, our dreams, etc.) is a detail from the experience of another present, past and/or future life. If you are open to this possibility, you will become aware of it. Your soul will direct you to this absolute knowledge if that is the plan you have chosen for this lifetime.

Chapter 24

Hybrids, yes, but on Earth?

The end of the day takes place in tranquility. We are all gathered in the living room of the condo we occupy on the edge of Crucita beach in Ecuador. Suddenly, my husband exclaims:

⏤ "Look, there! There's light!"

With excitement, he points to the horizon where something intriguing is held. About five to ten kilometers from us, blue-green, fluorescent light emanates from the depths of the ocean. It flashes with an energetic and regular rhythm, projecting a fantastic visual effect on the surface of the water. The movement of the waves spreads the beam over a width of more than 500 meters and creates the illusion of several lights underwater. However, there are no fishing boats in sight, the horizon offers no sign of a lighthouse or other source of light. It's unlike anything we've seen in the months we've spent by the ocean.

Being all spellbound, our gaze is fixed on this distinct glow during the sunset. It is inconceivable that the orientation of the rays could produce this phenomenon: it literally looks like the heart of the ocean beating from its depths. And then, slowly, everything disappears. The entire evening is dedicated to finding explanations for what we all saw at the same time. We go to bed without any of us being able to understand what has happened. In the stillness of the night, the Beings of Light descend into my dreams, eager to explain what we have witnessed. In my consciousness, they convey their message to me:

⏤ "We are here, in Crucita. It is time for you to know about our existence in this place. It's not just a coincidence that you're here right now. You are destined to be here, because everything is planned in what you have chosen to live. Very close to the underwater base where the portal is located, is our sanctuary where we protect and nourish hybrid Beings. They have become an integral part of our civilization and yours. We ensure their survival because you will need them in the near future. A global event is taking place. We are very concerned about the survival of humans. Our goal is to preserve your planet and ensure your well-being. You don't have to worry."

Frightened by the content of this exchange, I wake up. It is three o'clock in the morning. Worried, I need support. In addition, such messages tend to fade from my memory when I wake up. I wake up my husband to share with him what has just been disclosed. He too is taken aback by what I reveal to him. The next day, our intrigued minds are filled with multiple questions. My husband is looking for information about similar events in Crucita. He finds an interview with Jaime Rodriguez, a prominent ufologist from Ecuador, who discusses unusual activities in the surrounding waters. This corroborates the fascinating otherworldly connection to this village.

For me, a burning question always arises: why create hybrid beings? What is the link with the survival of the human species? Almost immediately, I start receiving downloads that contain answers. In this globally uncertain phase of our journey on Earth, I have a duty to share these revelations with you. The following information is transmitted telepathically:

⏤ "A group of benevolent, compassionate, and far-sighted Beings have recognized that the human population is facing a threat. The decrease or alteration of DNA puts the survival of humanity in a precarious balance. Determined to protect us, they have developed a plan to ensure the survival of your species and the preservation of your beloved planet."

⏤ "We have encountered similar problems with other planets in the past. We are determined to prevent history from repeating itself. We are unable to create beings who are fully human, but we do have the ability to delve into their essence and understand their wholeness. So, we fashioned hybrids by merging beings of our species with humans. To do this, a human woman carries the hybrid embryo until it is formed and able to exist outside the womb (about ten weeks). For these women, this can manifest as a feeling of bloating, heaviness, or even movement in the lower abdomen. They may have a vague feeling that something has been removed from their body. Sometimes their hormonal cycles are disrupted for a while."

For my part, between the ages of 17 and 25, I experienced these uncomfortable manifestations at times. Years later, I make connections to the hybrid nursery in the spaceship that I had witnessed at the age six. I now understand the experience of my pregnant mother, lying on a bed, surrounded by Beings of Light. Without certain proof, it is very likely that I was one of the volunteers destined to give birth to hybrids. And my mom. Assured, the Beings of Light inform me that we can put an end to it. Immediately, I declare that this contract ceases instantly for my lineage so that my children are not bound by transgenerational obligations. Once removed from their mother's womb, the baby hybrids are placed in containers, filled with a thick, nourishing liquid. They are connected to music and sounds that are part of the Language of the Stars. To develop and nourish the human fiber, some of you have volunteered. The volunteers leave their earthly shells while they sleep to come aboard the spaceship. They care for the hybrid babies by cuddling and rocking them.

As for men, their liquid is collected and kept for later use.

In this hybrid development project, several experiments have been carried out. A momentous lesson that the Beings of Light have learned is that the survival of these hybrid beings depends on the love and affection of humans. From this realization, they continually sought out subjects of our kind willing to fulfill this mission. Individuals who have accepted and do not remember will continue this role. It seems that this cycle of volunteering spans several generations. The term will end when someone declares that it is over. Future lines are automatically freed from it. My mother, who often ventured into other dimensions at night, shares these ideas. She revealed that she was scared during one of her trips. She decided to stop these explorations, fearing that she would not be able to return to Earth and take care of us.

I realize that unconsciously, as men and women, we play a role in the sustainability of our civilization. Several individuals have signed the contract to procreate hybrid beings. And since there are hybrids on every continent, what is the real number of humans on the planet? Who is hybrid, who is 100% human? There are non-humans of non-terrestrial origin who have borrowed a body like you and me and who have been with us for a very long time...

In the midst of integrating this information, which gives meaning to the experience that go back more than 40 years, the downloads continue:

⊢ "As a sign of our commitment to the progress of civilization on Earth, we are unveiling strategies that have been implemented for thousands of years. Yes, we are involved in what you call abductions. It is essential that you understand that these actions are motivated solely by our concern for your survival. Our intention is to deepen knowledge of the subtleties of human behavior: its relational exchanges, its emotions, and its reactions. This process allows us to create hybrid beings. As we repeat, our goal is to ensure the evolution of your species. So that we are able to figure out how to support you through the stages at this incoherent step of your humanity. Our preparations are already in place and actions have begun. We recognize that negative experiences, abuse, or psychological trauma have unfortunately been endured by many humans. However, these situations were not orchestrated by us. In the nature of all things, the dark side is represented. The ones with lower vibrations. There are different groups of Grey Beings. The Grey Beings who have chosen this path have made agreements with influential authorities on your planet. In exchange for advanced technological knowledge, this malevolent clan was allowed to conduct experiments that caused harm. However, it is essential to keep in mind that there are benevolent Grey Beings. In concrete terms, they are similar to your species. After witnessing the destruction and disappearance of their own planet, they came here to serve as educators. Their mission is to guide you and show you the importance of protecting the planet and how it works. If you encounter such Beings, it is probably part of your contract to help humanity and contribute to the emergence of the New Earth.

My further investigation into the purpose of creating hybrids reveals a stark truth: many among the population are unaware of the disturbing and rapid spread of a harmful substance, which may have already infiltrated the body unknowingly. This threat is perpetrated by those who seek the destruction of our species, but it goes unnoticed by the people who continue to exist in a dormant state. This passive existence, which is similar to robotic behavior, serves as the backdrop for the matrix. The system in which people have been trapped since birth even extends through the various lifetimes they have spent on Earth.

Many men and women let themselves be lulled by conformism. They get lost in captivating distractions that have been purposely designed to maintain their hypnotic state. There are those who progress without conscience or with indifference. Other individuals, like you and me, are summoned by an inner call: the vibration in their soul. More and more of us are recognizing a huge transformation that is taking place on Earth. A return to what was is impossible. This awareness calls for action, each in his or her own way, for the good of all humanity.

In a few words, the human race is experiencing a gradual decline. Though, the population of Light entities supports humanity by guiding them on the path forward, to ensure a better world and a better future. In some cases, planets have faced disintegration, with populations too small and insufficiently conscious to raise vibrations in order to save their place of life. Hybrids are a key to continuing the evolution of these planets, including our own. All this helps to understand the multitude of dimensions that coexist. The fate of future generations depends on these actions. Each soul has the freedom to take the direction it desires to live. Time will bear witness to the unfolding of the changes related to our choices in the here and now.

Chapter 25

Dreams and a parallel life

The Ecuadorian Andes lull my senses on this comfortable night. Rest is welcome after a busy day. I quickly slip into sleep. A dream awaits me. In this other reality, I glance at my watch. The figures displayed are unknown to me. I head outside. The cool wind makes the sides of the alpaca wool poncho in which I am draped sway. In the middle of the sky, a gigantic navy-blue portal appears that I recognize. Luminous shapes emerge from it and begin their descent. Countless spaceships are now all around. Appearing out of nowhere, thousands of panicked children rush in all directions. I feel they are disoriented and anxious. In a remarkably fast sequence, transparent, shiny tubes descend from the vessels onto the children. As soon as they are inside, they disappear. The dream ends with the aura dust they leave behind.

I wake up with the memory of the children's distress. Troubled, I have the impression that it is a premonition. The heavy sorrow of my intuition fades. A few moments later, a warmth takes place in my body. I feel a great peace. It comes from the children who have now arrived in the City of Light. In addition, I still have trouble sleeping the following days. It is a vision that will remain engraved in my memory for a long time.

About seven years later, the rest of the dream occurs. We are on vacation in the Canadian Rockies. This time, I have a broader overview. I witness the arrival of the spaceships not only on Earth, but also in a spacious valley surrounded by crystal clear and sparkling waters of elsewhere. I see children, animals, insects, lush vegetation, fruits, and vegetables at will. It is a paradise where young souls connect with all aspects of the environment. The whole thing looks like the City of Light. The spirit of cooperation and mutual aid reigns supreme. The children's guides and elders are selected according to a specific criterion of awakening: to recognize that their previous lives were only illusions. As I watch the scene, I notice that the children are learning to take care of animals, take care of the land and create beautiful gardens. They discover the art of making clothes from cotton plants and making objects from elements available in nature. It is a true vision of unity, growth, and enlightenment.

Identical as in the initial dream, many spaceships appear. My intuition tells me that these are extensions of the City of Light. The children, completely transformed and reprogrammed, land through the same tubes with which they boarded the spaceship the first time. With an inner calm, they are joyful and radiant. I am convinced that the vessel came to get me, my family and other people chosen to go to the City of Light. The time has come to make the transition to this new dimension. This idea fills me with excitement and joy.

When I wake up, the sensations are opposite to the first dream. Hope and effervescence circulate in my being. Taking a step back, I associate the tragedy felt at first thought with the arrival of the highly advertised (and unfortunately obligatory in many situations) substance linked to the global pandemic of 2020. This event that affected the entire globe: as tumultuous as it was, served as a catalyst for humanity to see the world from a new perspective.

To me, it has awakened the recognition that there are worlds and dimensions waiting to be explored. Just like the children of my dreams, let us keep our eyes and hearts riveted on the sky, amazed. Despite this hope, I recognize that for many, a veil remains over the City of Light. This veil thickens because people give up their power in the hundreds of daily distractions and stimulations.

My dreams have imparted to me the knowledge that the emergence of the New Earth will take place when humanity frees itself from its own blinders. The limitless potential is still there, on the other side of the curtain. Dear reader, you who are in the middle of a moment of awakening in life, you are an inspiration. You are examples of those who are taking back their power. Continue to embrace the infinite wonders of existence!

The path to the City of Light

The more humanity awakens, the more it progresses towards this new state of existence. In all parts of the Earth, people are attracted to each other. Meetings are multiplying. Through these interactions, connections take shape and allow for a radiant transformation within each individual. The activated inner light helps sweep away negativity. Along the way, we rub shoulders with people who have chosen to stay in the current vibrations. Little by little, these people disappear from our path, as if they had never existed. The density of the planet is thus lightened. Our eyes open to perceive the beauty of each Being. The true nature of those we consider scary or strange will surface. Our minds, until then limited to perceiving the visible, will undergo a remarkable change: seeing the invisible and the beyond. The City of Light is emerging with increasing strength. The veil that envelops our perception is slowly lifting for those who have an open heart.

My journey is far from lonely. A collective of individuals like me have chosen to make a difference in this momentous period. People around the world are channeling their gifts and talents to reprogram particular individuals who play a central role in supporting humanity. Or they reprogram the DNA of those who are destined to embark on the path to the City of Light. Others are chosen to support and guide the future generation, towards a brighter and more harmonious future. Awareness and implementation of its mission is the story of a lifetime. Listening to what is greater than oneself is actualized in various ways. Including people who help animals, plants, and other living organisms. It is a question of following one's feelings, freeing oneself from one's limitations and remaining open to exploring alternative paths.

The journey may have been shaped by many psychological traumas. These are trials and tests of strength, resilience, and adaptation. They reflect the challenges that the children faced when they arrived in the City of Light. All this was done in order to be ready to assume the role one has chosen for oneself in the manifestation of the New World that is looming on the horizon...

The bridge

To live in the City of Light, it is necessary to be mentally, physically, and psychologically strong. It is also essential to be ready to transcend the limits of earthly life. Our bitter or traumatic stories become burdens that we carry throughout our journey. With no sparing in their lives, even if people are among the first to arrive near the bridge leading to the City of Light, they will be the last to cross. On this bridge, there is an energetic purge of all the lives that are happening at the same time. There follows a destabilizing loss of reference points for those who have not done any inner work. This upgrade is necessary to tune in to the vibrational frequencies of the New Earth, which are very different from the current third dimension of our planet. The sufferings of the past are dissipating. Some individuals may even go into a deep sleep lasting three to four days while their body completes the adaptation.

The environment of this advanced civilization is nothing but unconditional love. It's absolutely wonderful. Now freed from our scars, the energetic bath of love transforms us by gradually erasing our identity. Only the connection with the essence of our ancestors of all our lives and dimensions remains. The path to the City of Light is a journey of deep healing for another, an even greater kind of awakening.

Chapter 26

Conclusion

Ordinary, like everyone else

I was born into a very ordinary life, in a family like so many others. At the time, I only spoke French and didn't consider myself popular at school. I had few friends, and I followed the school career with difficulties. My great-grandparents bestowed me some special abilities as gifts. They brought me the label of "black sheep" of the family (which remains the same today…but it's of no importance to me anymore!) I didn't feel different from the others. As a defense mechanism, my brain temporarily cut off access to my childhood experiences. On the other hand, I also believed that everyone saw what I saw including the deceased. I didn't feel any better than others when I started to realize that wasn't the case and when, later, I saw the City of Light. I was struggling with time-consuming questions. My journey is an example of how an ordinary person, like me, can choose to participate in this mission that we all have: that of evolving. We are here to learn and become what we have set out to be to help, in our own way, to move humanity and life on Earth forward.

I am who I am today thanks to all the tests of life that have presented themselves at the right time. From my earliest childhood memories, I have been in communion with my ancestors. Without understanding the meaning at the time, countless challenges have been carefully designed and dropped in my journey by my Beings of Light. When I was six years old, I was a student on the spaceship. When I was fifteen, I saw the City of Light for the first time. At the age of 36, with the birth of my children, my mission became more precise. Interactions with my Beings of Light have developed and deepened. At the beginning of my forties, I discovered my gift of the Language of the Stars. Its evolution has continued since then. Information and downloads added up over time. All this allows me to understand the enigmatic moments I have lived since my childhood. These trials have helped me to grasp my deep identity and what is an integral part of who I am. I have frequently asked myself: why me? Why did I have adventures with such irrational revelations in the current system? In a discussion with my editor, I repeated this same question. She spontaneously replied:

― "Anick, you experienced them because you have the ability to remember it all. The goal is to share to make known what is always present and invisible for the moment. By revealing your story, everything will become more and more visible."

Strangely enough, I hadn't looked at it that way. Her response had the effect of a nice surprise. I am sure I was chosen because I represent the vast majority of ordinary people around the world. At least, those of us who yearn for peace, love, and unity on our planet. While feeling lucky, it's more of a duty to share this knowledge with the world. One thing is certain: I am not alone in the world. Many people like me exist but have chosen to remain discreet. Given the unreal nature of these experiences, one can understand their choice.

Other people around the world have compiled their experiences into a book like I do. However, they may not have had the courage to speak their truth so openly. I am aware that not everyone shares the same vision as me. And that's fine! What really matters is to be authentic to oneself and pass on the knowledge that has been entrusted to me.

Life is like a gigantic stage in which a play takes place in which we all have a role to play according to our essence. It's up to us to make choices. Who do we invite into our lives? How do we react to what does or does not come to us? Who takes on the role of director? What are the themes that define our lives?

Immerse yourself in wonder, vibrate with the joy of living this life surrounded by mysteries. Believe in yourself, your presence has a reason. The path to be taken is up to you to define. Walk the path of your destiny with audacity!

For me, this life is great. It is an incredible opportunity, rich in infinite possibilities intertwined with the world of Energy. My deepest and heartfelt gratitude goes out to the unseen forces of Light that have been comforting, supporting, guiding, and inspiring me since my arrival into this world.

Anick Bourbonnière

To find out more or to contact the author,

Website : www.lightlanguage.co

E-mail : ttakbourbonniere@hotmail.com

Editor's final comment:

Evelyne Delude

In 2020, when I discovered Anick's Language of the Stars for the first time, I was scared! In the space of a second, I felt something unravel inside the solar plexus. My brain got involved and fear came up. I stopped the video and closed everything. During the next day, I took up only an excerpt from the Language of the Stars. The feeling was quite different. Soothed and rested, I felt bigger than the limits of my body. Immediately, I told Anick about my experience by email. Without delay, her answer reached me: "I understand you, it's quite normal!" Wanting to know more, I treated myself to a few sessions with Anick. Supported by the Language of the Stars and letting time do its work, transformations took place in me.

I have been working mainly with children identified on the autism spectrum in schools for more than 25 years. In a system that was running out of steam, I wondered if I still had a place there. Regardless of the scenarios, my reflections inevitably brought me back to the same point: supporting children in their development is still what I do best and what drives me the most. Anick kept telling me the same thing: "You have an incredible mission here." But I still had to find a way to do it differently...

Collaborating on this book has allowed me to better understand the reality of children with special needs. My perceptions have become more refined, my energy has changed. In the course of writing, I had the confirmation that I was fully updating my mission while becoming aware of its scope. Since the beginning of my career, the warriors of Gaia and I have joined forces. I sometimes even have the impression that some people have chosen me. At least, the crossroads of our paths is not the result of chance.